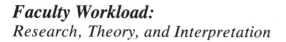
Faculty Workload:
Research, Theory, and Interpretation

by Harold E. Yuker

ASHE-ERIC Higher Education Research Report No. 10, 1984

INDEX ISSUE, 1984 SERIES

Prepared by

 ® *Clearinghouse on Higher Education*
The George Washington University

Published by

ASHE

Association for the Study of Higher Education

Jonathan D. Fife,
Series Editor

Cite as:
Yuker, Harold E. *Faculty Workload: Research, Theory, and Interpretation*. ASHE-ERIC Higher Education Research Report No. 10. Washington, D.C.: Association for the Study of Higher Education, 1984.

The ERIC Clearinghouse on Higher Education invites individuals to submit proposals for writing monographs for the Higher Education Research Report series. Proposals must include:
1. A detailed manuscript proposal of not more than five pages.
2. A 75-word summary to be used by several review committees for the initial screening and rating of each proposal.
3. A vita.
4. A writing sample.

Library of Congress Catalog Card Number: 85-62067
ISSN 0737-1292
ISBN 0-913317-19-5

ᴱᴿᴵᶜ® Clearinghouse on Higher Education
The George Washington University
One Dupont Circle, Suite 630
Washington, D.C. 20036

ASHE Association for the Study of Higher Education
One Dupont Circle, Suite 630
Washington, D.C. 20036

This publication was partially prepared with funding from the National Institute of Education, U.S. Department of Education under contract no. 400-82-0011. The opinions expressed in this report do not necessarily reflect the positions or policies of NIE or the Department.

EXECUTIVE SUMMARY

This monograph updates earlier summaries of information pertaining to faculty workload (Bunnell 1960; Stecklein 1961; Yuker 1974) and integrates data obtained in earlier studies with more recent information.

Faculty workload refers to all faculty activities that are related to professional duties and responsibilities: teaching, research, interacting with students, institutional service, service to the community, and professional development. These data are used in collective bargaining, cost analyses, equity analyses, grant proposals, lawmaking and lawsuits, budgeting, and publicizing the nature of faculty duties (Bleything 1982; Lorents 1971; Stecklein 1961, 1974).

Data pertaining to workload can be obtained from institutional reports citing statistics relating to student credit hours, student credit hours per full-time equivalent faculty, faculty contact hours, and student/faculty ratios. Although formulas that weight each type of faculty activity have been developed (Henle 1967; Miller 1968), they often are not satisfactory.

Information about workload can be obtained from faculty members' indications of the amounts of time they devote to instruction, research, institutional service, public service, professional development, student advisement, and so on. In such surveys, problems may arise pertaining to the classes of activities used and the accuracy of the data obtained. Surveys of faculty members must be carefully planned and decisions made about the sample to be used, its size, when to administer the survey, the time period to be covered, and the instructions given about allocating time (Lorents 1971; Ritchey 1959; Romney 1971; Stecklein 1961; Thomas 1982). The researcher must decide whether to use questionnaires, diaries, interviews, work samples, or a combination of techniques. Faculty members should be involved in planning the study, and they should be informed of the purpose of the study and its benefits to them and to their department. Care must be taken to ensure that the data obtained are both reliable and valid.

Instructional time, which includes time spent in class, in preparing for class, and in evaluating students, varies as a function of several factors: More time is devoted to instruction in developing than in developed nations. Teaching loads tend to be lowest at research universities and highest at community colleges (Fulton and Trow 1974;

Ladd and Lipset 1977; Stecklein, Willie, and Lorenz 1983). Variations among disciplines are generally not great because most institutions have universitywide regulations that apply to most departments.

Myths abound concerning the time devoted to specific courses. Data indicate, however, that it is not influenced by the size of the class, the level of the course, or the number of different course preparations, except that initial preparations take more time than subsequent ones. Rank influences teaching load; at most institutions full professors have the lightest teaching loads, instructors the heaviest. Individual differences in interest in teaching compared to research or other activities tend to result in variations in the amount of time devoted to instructional activities, even when faculty members have identical teaching loads.

Most studies of workload combine research, scholarship, and creative activities in a broad category that includes all behaviors aimed at producing a scholarly work like a book, article, painting, musical composition, or recital. Data indicate that these types of "research productivity" are primarily influenced by interest and past experience and *not* by teaching load; reduced load usually does not result in increased research productivity.

Although every campus has productive researchers and faculty members who produce no scholarly output, productive scholars tend to be more prevalent at "high-quality" institutions (Fulton and Trow 1974; Ladd and Lipset 1977). Scholarly productivity tends to be relatively high in the sciences and social sciences and low in the humanities and arts. Full professors tend to be the most productive, instructors and assistant professors the least productive. While differences in productivity between genders have been found, they disappear when variables such as institutional type, discipline, and rank are parceled out. Individual differences in research interest account for much of the variance in differences in productivity.

The amount of time that faculty members devote to activities other than teaching and research varies greatly. Many faculty members engage in some type of remunerative off-campus activity—teaching at another institution, consulting, engaging in private practice, or giving lectures, for example. Faculty members devote from about 3 percent to over 20 percent of their time to meetings and administrative activities, with full professors devoting the most time. Individual differences result in wide variations in the amount of time devoted to professional development, such as keeping up with the literature, attending disciplinary meetings, conventions, and conferences, and taking courses.

Hundreds of studies over many years yield convergent data indicating that faculty members report that they devote an average of 55 hours per week during the academic year to professional activities. The 55-hour week conforms to data reported by lawyers, doctors, and business executives. Studies based upon methods other than faculty reports indicate that an average of 45 hours may be more appropriate if the hours devoted to personal activities are excluded. Faculty members interested in research are more apt to spend time working during the summer than are those primarily interested in teaching.

The data relating institutional type to total workload indicate that faculty at research universities tend to put in more hours per week than those at other types of institutions (Fulton and Trow 1974). Faculty members in the higher ranks report that they work a few more hours per week than those in the lower ranks. Male faculty members report that they work slightly more hours than females. But all of these group differences are insignificant compared to individual differences. At every institution, in every department, and in every rank, some faculty members work fewer than 30 hours a week while others work more than 70.

Most workload studies should be conducted under the aegis of a faculty/administration committee. They should be preceded by a thorough review of the literature and should be conducted by knowledgeable researchers. Presentation of the data should demonstrate recognition of differences among institutions, departments, and individuals. One way of doing so is by including measures of variability.

Researchers who study workload should be very careful in comparing institutions, departments, or individuals. These levels differ in many ways, tending to make comparisons inappropriate. Workload data can be used to individualize faculty contracts so that they reflect faculty members' interests. The complexity of the relationship between teaching load, teaching effectiveness, and scholarly productivity must be recognized. Neither institutions nor faculty members should assume that changes in assigned teaching load will lead to changes in research or teaching productivity. Finally, studies demonstrating the validity of faculty workload surveys are needed.

Virginia B. Nordby
Director
Affirmative Action Programs
University of Michigan

Harold Orlans
Office of Programs and Policy
United States Civil Rights Commission

Lois S. Peters
Center for Science and Technology Policy
New York University

John M. Peterson
Director, Technology Planning
The B. F. Goodrich Company

Marianne Phelps
Assistant Provost for Affirmative Action
The George Washington University

Richard H. Quay
Social Science Librarian
Miami University

John E. Stecklein
Professor of Educational Psychology
University of Minnesota

Donald Williams
Professor of Higher Education
University of Washington

CONTENTS

FOREWORD

Faculty workload studies are either unused or underutilized at many institutions because of a general resistance from both administrators and faculty members. There is a shared skepticism about the reliability of such studies. Administrators feel that self-reported studies are suspect and the data inflated; faculty may acknowledge the accuracy of the data but not the possibility of meaningfully comparing such subgroups as the humanities and the sciences, or even various academic ranks. In general, faculty also feel that they are above workload studies, which have connotations of Federick Taylor's assembly line studies of time and motion.

Academic resistance to workload studies is understandable not because of faulty methodology, but because of poorly conceived applications. These studies should not be used to look at performance of individual faculty members since other methods more appropriately evaluate faculty performance by the results of their work rather than a per-hour accounting. Workload studies are best used when they are weighed against the institution's mission and goals. Of course for studies to be effective the institutional mission and individual subunit goals must be articulated to a level of specificity that parallels workload activities.

Workload study data can be gathered for evidence that will answer the following questions:

- Are faculty members dividing their time in a way that is consistent with the general mission of the institution?
- On the whole, does there appear to be inappropriate emphasis in areas that are inconsistent with or dysfunctional to the institution's mission?
- Within specific academic subunits is there an appropriate balance of workload activity, keeping in mind that one academic subunit may vary greatly from another? Are workload activities at different academic ranks appropriate and consistent with institutional goals and missions?

Workload studies can be used to answer these and other questions to determine whether faculty time is appropriately allocated. If not, an analysis can determine the reasons. Is there something wrong with hiring policies? Do the norms of the disciplines differ too greatly from the institutional mission? Will certain incentives promote the appropriate workload emphasis? A careful analysis can (1) identify reasons for the workload emphasis and (2) suggest new procedures or incentives to encourage desired change. In other words, the mission and goals of an institution are achieved primarily through the faculty. Without a clear understanding of how the faculty spend their time, there cannot be an understanding of why goals are or are not being achieved and in what areas change is needed.

In this report by Harold E. Yuker, Mervyn L. Schloss Distinguished Professor and Director of the Center for the Study of Attitudes Towards Persons with Disabilities at Hofstra University, the full concept of faculty workload studies is reviewed. This thorough examination by Dr. Yuker provides the basis for institutions to develop more effective workload studies that will achieve reliable information for the institution and avoid repeating the mistakes that so often have occurred in the past.

Jonathan D. Fife
Series Editor
Professor and Director
ERIC Clearinghouse on Higher Education
The George Washington University

ACKNOWLEDGMENTS

I wish to thank the many persons who helped in the preparation of this manuscript. ERIC provided an initial list of references. My graduate assistant, Michael Hurley, and the staff of the Hofstra University library were very helpful and managed to provide copies of everything I requested. My secretary, Ruth Mangels, was a big help in typing the manuscript.

My sincere thanks to Dr. Everett C. Ladd, Executive Director of the Roper Center at the University of Connecticut, for making the data from the 1977 Ladd and Lipset study available to me. These new data have added a significant dimension to this report.

The final version of this monograph has benefited from the constructive comments of three colleagues. I have learned much from David Klein, now retired as a professor of sociology from Michigan State, who has been providing constructive criticisms of my manuscripts for 30 years. The ongoing friendship and support of James M. Shuart, president of Hofstra University, has been invaluable, and I wish to thank him for taking the time to read and comment on the manuscript. The comments of my good friend and severest critic, J. Richard Block, professor of psychology and assistant to the president at Hofstra University, were both annoying and very helpful. The monograph also benefited from the constructive comments of three anonymous reviewers.

FACULTY WORKLOAD: CONCEPTS AND USES

An increasing number of studies of faculty workload have been published in the years since the initial study by Koos (1919). Interest in these studies has waxed and waned over the years, tending to be highest when institutions of higher education face financial problems. All types of institutions, from two-year institutions to graduate and professional schools, have conducted the studies. Some have been poorly done, often because they were undertaken without adequate review of the literature discussing procedures and the results of prior research. In 1919, faculty workload tended to be influenced by "tradition, sentiment, rules of thumb, temporizing, and compromise" (Koos 1919, p. 5), and that is still the case. The present monograph provides information that can help improve the quality of studies of faculty workload.

Faculty workload tend[s] to be influenced by "tradition, sentiment, rules of thumb, temporizing, and compromise."

Definitions

A major problem in studies of faculty workload is deciding which faculty activities should be included in "workload" and which should be excluded. A narrow definition of workload might refer to only the number of assigned teaching hours or their equivalent in other activities. Most definitions are broad, however, and include all activities that take the time of a college or university teacher and are related directly or indirectly to professional duties, responsibilities, and interests (Stickler 1960). It includes preparation for teaching, classroom instruction, constructing and scoring examinations, reading and grading papers, research and/or creative work, directing graduate theses and dissertations, providing professional services, guidance and counseling, administrative duties, professional reading, committee work, and participation in extracurricular activities.

The inclusion of time spent in noninstructional activities sometimes causes problems. Everyone agrees that teaching, preparing for class, and evaluating students' performance are part of the teaching load. "The disagreement centers around such functions as research, professional writing, membership in professional organizations, routine correspondence, committee membership, advisor duties, and sponsorship duties" (Sexson 1967, p. 219). Sexson has overstated the case, however, because writers generally agree that committee membership, student advisement, and sponsorship of a dissertation are part of faculty load. The problems arise with respect to activities that appear to be more related to personal professional development than to normal assigned institutional duties. If a data processing manager reads a professional magazine at work, for example, it is part of his job; if he reads it at home, it is professional development and not specifically part of his job (Lorents 1971). But faculty members have freedom to spend their professional time wherever and whenever they wish. Thus, criteria other than time and place are necessary to determine whether or not a specific activity is considered part of a faculty member's total workload.

Theoretically, "the entire time and efforts of full-time staff members should be given to the institution" (Reeves et al. 1933, p. 270); thus, if one assumes faculty members are paid adequate salaries, all outside income resulting from their services should be paid to the university that has paid for all of their time. Although it would upset the many faculty members who supplement their salaries through outside teaching, speeches, consulting, and so forth, such a policy was in effect at the University of Chicago for a number of years.

Uses of Workload Data
Data on faculty workload are used in a number of ways: collective bargaining, cost analysis, equity, grant proposals, legal and legislative matters, and public relations (see, for example, Bleything 1982; Doi 1961; Eagleton 1977; Fairchild 1981; Hauck 1969; Henle 1967; Hill 1969; Lorents 1971; Romney 1971; Stecklein 1961, 1974).

Collective bargaining
An early study of workload provisions in collective bargaining agreements led to several conclusions:

- Workload provisions are not of crucial importance to unions.
- Workload provisions at two-year institutions tend to be more detailed than those at four-year institutions.
- Collective bargaining has resulted in neither increased workload nor increased productivity.
- Nonteaching activities are important parts of total workload.

- Workload provisions often specify how assignments are made and by whom (Mortimer and Lozier 1974).

A later study of workload provisions in collective bargaining agreements concluded that although teaching load continues to be the most important item, the number of teaching items included in more recent bargaining agreements has decreased, rather than increased, as Mortimer and Lozier predicted (Creswell, Kramer, and Newton 1978).

Workload provisions in collective bargaining agreements may give faculty members more control over their individual assignments—whether they teach graduate or undergraduate courses, small or large classes, lectures or seminars, for example (Naples, Caruthers, and Naples 1978). Institutions with collective bargaining agreements usually cannot increase faculty workloads unless they also increase salaries (Naples, Caruthers, and Naples 1978). The impression that total faculty workloads are lower at unionized institutions has not been documented in the literature.

Collective bargaining agreements tend to specify minimum and/or maximum workloads (Goeres 1978). Minimum workloads are defined for the benefit of the employer, maximum workloads for the benefit of faculty. Many collective bargaining agreements define workload in general terms, involving a combination of teaching, research, university service, and public service. Others are more complex and define specific tasks.

Cost analysis
In preparing budgets at institutions of higher education, data on teaching load can be combined with data on tuition to yield a type of cost/benefit analysis. These data are important as faculty salaries constitute a significant share of the budgets of institutions of higher education (Bleything 1982; Yarborough 1982). At an average institution, faculty salaries account for 25 percent of the budget, other personnel costs for 32 percent, and other expenses for 43 percent (Bowen 1980). The cost of faculty began to accelerate in the late 1950s, and the acceleration continued through the 1960s and 1970s (Mayhew 1979). At many institutions, the increase is the result of more faculty in the upper ranks and a reduction in teaching loads.

To survive the institutional retrenchment of the 1980s, many colleges and universities would have to increase faculty members' teaching loads, class size, and student/faculty ratios (Mayhew 1979). Others have suggested reducing faculty members' teaching loads accompanied by a proportionate reduction in salary and sharing loads between two faculty members (Ayre et al. 1981).

Equity

Data obtained in studies of workload can be used to demonstrate the presence or lack of equity. Junior and senior faculty members may eye one another with suspicion, members of each group convinced that members of the other are not doing their share of the work (Starr 1973). The same suspicion may exist between female and male faculty members, and among departments, divisions, and schools. Frequently, faculty perceive that others (particularly faculty members in schools of law and medicine) are receiving more money for less work. As *perceptions* of inequality can result in impaired performance, they need to be attended to (Naples, Caruthers, and Naples 1978). Carefully conducted studies of workload can confirm or disprove perceptions of inequity.

Grant proposals

The 1979 Office of Management and Budget Circular A-21, which set standards to be used in setting indirect costs for government-sponsored research, requires strict accounting for the percentage of time that faculty members devote to government-sponsored research as opposed to other duties. This requirement elicited negative reactions from faculty members, who were concerned by the possibility that the data would be inaccurate and by the fact that time and effort that could be devoted to research would have to be spent compiling data (Shulman 1980). When the regulations were issued, Stanford University responded by requiring *all* faculty members to complete quarterly reports accounting for all of their work time (*Chronicle of Higher Education* 22 October 1979). Circular A-21 was revised and made somewhat more flexible in 1982; the requirement that 100 percent of a faculty member's time must be accounted for was removed.

Legal and legislative matters

Many states have rules pertaining to the workloads of faculty members in public institutions of higher education just as they have rules pertaining to teachers in elementary and secondary schools. In one study, 36 states indicated they were collecting data on faculty workload from public institutions (Huther 1974). Some states base appropriations for state colleges and universities upon measures of productivity like faculty workload. In another survey, 19 states required data on workload from postsecondary institutions, more than half of those that did not require it were discussing it, and 90 percent of the states indicated they would probably raise the issue in state legislatures during the 1980s (Henard 1979). The impression is widespread among legislators that faculty members have easy jobs involving working only a few hours a week, nine months of the year (Henard 1979).

The importance of an accurate definition of faculty workload has emerged in court cases involving the definition of what constitutes half-time teaching in connection with membership in a collective bargaining unit. An interesting brief dealing with this subject (Geeter 1981) notes the difficulty in defining faculty workload in terms of contact hours. Previous court decisions recognized that a definition of 20 hours per week as constituting half-time work is not adequate for college teaching because the amount of time a faculty member spends in class constitutes only the "tip of the iceberg." The university involved argued that research, supervising a dissertation, academic committee work, and attending professional meetings all constitute important parts of a faculty member's total workload and that teaching load by itself is consequently not synonymous with workload.

Public relations

Many people have little understanding of what college professors do. They hear that faculty members teach six to 12 hours a week, eight or nine months a year, realize that occasional papers must be graded, and may have heard of the need to publish or perish, but it still seems to be an easy job. When they hear of studies revealing that college faculty claim to work an average of 55 hours per week, most people, including many faculty members and administrators, are openly skeptical. In view of this skepticism—especially among legislators and government officials—that can affect attempts to obtain financial support for higher education, it is necessary to educate the public about the duties and the long work hours of faculty members.

Studying Faculty Workload

To study faculty workload, one must first answer several procedural questions (Manning and Romney 1973; Stecklein 1961): defining the purpose of the study, defining workload and categories of workload, and selecting the methodology to be employed. (These questions are discussed in greater detail in the following chapters.)

Every study should start with the preparation of a statement of purpose because both the procedures used and the extent of faculty cooperation depend upon the purpose of the study. The researchers must specify the questions they are trying to answer and the uses to be made of the data. Once the purposes are established, they should be widely circulated among the faculty members who will be participating in the study to obtain their cooperation.

Next, the researchers should provide a precise and operational definition of workload. Is workload defined by the number of courses taught, by the number of credit hours taught, by the number of students taught, or by some other measure? Should one count the number of committee memberships or the number of hours spent in committee meetings? Which activities should be included and which excluded? Should time devoted to professional reading, to attending meetings with local officials or businessmen, or to a leisurely friendly lunch with colleagues be included?

Next, the researcher must resolve problems relating to the designation and definition of workload categories. How many types of activities should be specified? What types of activities are most important? How can the categories be defined clearly and concisely so that all faculty members interpret them uniformly?

Then questions of methodology arise. How should the population be defined? Should it include teaching assistants, full-time researchers, part-time administrators? Should one study the entire faculty or just a sample? What time period should be studied: two weeks, a month, a full year? Should the data be obtained as an estimate before or after the fact, or should a diary be used? What are the advantages of diaries compared to interviews? Whose cooperation is needed?

Finally, the researcher must decide whether to use institutional measures or to survey the faculty. Institutional measures are those that most institutions of higher education routinely collect. They include measures of student credit hours, student contact hours, and student/faculty ratios. Although these data are usually easily generated, they have a number of faults.

Well-done faculty surveys yield much more data and can be more useful, but they require much more time and effort. Problems relating to each of these techniques are discussed in the following chapters.

WORKLOAD DATA FROM INSTITUTIONAL REPORTS

Some data pertaining to faculty workload can be extracted from administrative surveys routinely made at many institutions of higher education. Statistics yielded by such reports often provide information about student credit hours (SCHs), faculty contact hours, and student/faculty ratios. These types of data are sometimes used in faculty workload formulas.

Student Credit Hours
Faculty workload is usually defined in terms of assigned credit hours. Some schools assign a 15-hour load, many have a 12-hour load, and some assign loads of six hours. Although a constant ratio between credit-hour load and total load is usually assumed, implying that credit-hour load gives a reliable index of total load (Stickler 1960), studies show that the total hours faculty work per credit hour varies from about two to about eight (Ayer 1929; Knowles and White 1939; Mitchell 1937; Stewart 1934; Woodburne 1958). Despite this evidence that credit hours are an inadequate measure of faculty workload, the use of credit hours has continued.

> *Clearly the conclusion of virtually all studies from 1929 to 1959 was that neither credit hour, contact hour, student hours, or student contact hours were by themselves, or together, reliable indicators of faculty members' workloads. Despite the results of these studies, the convenient descriptive load of fifteen credit hours per week (with an average of two hours preparation and grading for each credit hour taught) has persisted throughout higher education. . . . The use of the "credit hour" as a standard criterion for evaluating an individual's contribution to the work of his university is even less appropriate now than it was ten years ago and it was clearly inappropriate then* (Interuniversity Council 1970, p. 8).

A slightly more sophisticated approach is to multiply the number of credits assigned to a course by the number of students enrolled in the course to yield a measure of SCHs, which some institutions consider a good measure of faculty productivity. If the total SCHs for a given faculty member are multiplied by the tuition charged per credit, the result-

Despite . . . evidence that credit hours are an inadequate measure of faculty workload, the use of credit hours has continued.

ing number represents the income generated by the faculty member, which can then be compared to that person's salary. This method is still an oversimplification, however, and has the same faults as faculty credit hours.

Student Credit Hours per Full-Time Equivalent

Another approach, which Doi (1961) and Durham (1960) consider a good measure of the efficiency of both departments and individual faculty members, is to calculate the average number of student credit hours taught by faculty members by dividing the total number of student credit hours for a unit (department, school, or institution) by the number of full-time equivalent (FTE) faculty in that unit. If this measure were used as a standard, it would make possible comparisons among different departments, schools, or universities. Of course, comparisons can be made only when the data have been collected using similar definitions and similar techniques of collection (Durham 1960).

SCH/FTE is particularly useful as budgetary information. One can not only compare ratios of departments and institutions but also calculate the costs per student credit hour to indicate relative costs of programs. In 1957–58, for example, the comparative cost per SCH for institutions in the Montana system ranged from a low of $3.00 for psychology and philosophy at one school to a high of $95.83 for physical education at another school. At the University of Utah, the cost ranged from $4.47 per SCH in sociology to $285.00 in radiology (Durham 1960). More recent data from other schools show similarly wide variations.

Even though SCH/FTE is useful in budgeting, it has drawbacks as a measure of faculty workload. Because it concentrates on the instructional function of faculty, it ignores other activities such as research and administration (Toombs 1973). Consequently, it too is an unsatisfactory measure of total faculty productivity.

Contact Hours

Contact hours are defined as the number of (45- to 55-minute) hours that a faculty member spends teaching a class. Because the number of contact hours tends to be greater than the number of credit hours in courses that involve laboratories, studios, and physical education, in some institutions faculty members receive fewer credit hours for such courses. Faculty members who teach class hours requiring little or no preparation may receive only 50 percent to 75 percent of the contact hours as credit hours on their course load assignments (Lombardi 1974). On the other hand, credit hours may be greater than contact hours for courses in English composition or graduate courses, and course loads may be adjusted accordingly. The relationship between contact hours and credit hours can change as a result of faculty members' discontent, collective bargaining agreements, or other factors.

Contact hours rank second only to semester hours as a basis for defining load (National Education Association 1972a, 1972b). They are somewhat better than credit hours because they reflect work time rather than the arbitrary time indicated by credit hours, but they too tend to oversimplify the actual workload of faculty members and fail to reflect the complexity of faculty activities (Starr 1973).

On the positive side, the correlation between contact hours and total hours devoted to a course (including preparation, grading, and other activities) is higher than the correlation of any other measure with total course hours (Hesseldenz and Rodgers 1976). Thus, Hesseldenz and Rodgers concluded, contact hours are the best institutional measure of the amount of faculty effort devoted to a specific course. Although their data indicate that variables such as class size, class level, and faculty rank are unimportant, the information relates to a specific course, not to a faculty member's total workload.

As contact hours share many of the faults of credit hours, they too are unsatisfactory as measures of faculty workload.

Student/Faculty Ratio
While not generally used as a measure of faculty workload, student/faculty ratio is occasionally used as a measure of institutional quality, although little evidence indicates it is an accurate measure of either (Ruml and Morrison 1959). The ratio has been characterized as meaningless and "one of the most misleading indications of faculty load" (Hicks 1960, p. 9). The most reasonable approach might be to abandon faculty/student ratios until their utility has been demonstrated.

Thus, none of the institutional data are valid measures of faculty workload, and other types of measures must be used to get adequate data.

Formulas

A number of institutions have attempted to develop formulas to describe the workload of faculty members. The purpose of a formula is to develop equivalencies among such diverse tasks as teaching a course in freshman composition to 20 students, conducting a graduate seminar with three Ph.D. candidates in history, supervising an advanced-level chemistry laboratory, and serving as a reader on a doctoral dissertation committee. Some of the formulas are simple, involving few components (Hauck 1969; Hill 1969), others more complex (Henle 1967; Miller 1968).

Workload formulas differ greatly from one another with respect to the weights assigned to each component of workload. For example, in formulas that assigned different weights to lower-level and graduate-level courses and lower-level undergraduate courses were assigned a weight of 1.0, graduate courses were assigned weights of 1.4 (Miller 1968), 1.5 (Howell 1962), 2.0 (Banks 1963), 2.5 (Miller 1968), and 4.0 (Hill 1969). While one might expect some differences among institutions, one would hardly expect differences of this magnitude. Because the weights are arbitrary, they are meaningless. If they were based on data rather than theory, convergence would probably be more typical than large differences.

The many differences among the formulas should make one skeptical about their utility. Formulas ignore differences among faculty members and among different courses on the same level. For all of these reasons, workload formulas should be examined very critically before being considered for use.

The Utility of Institutional Data Measures

In theory, institutional data measures seem to be ideal. They are readily available from institutional records, so it is not necessary to survey the faculty. The definitions have been standardized so that problems of lack of understanding or use of different definitions do not exist. Further, most faculty contracts are based on one of these measures, the number of credit hours taught.

In practice, however, these measures are inadequate because their use involves several questionable assumptions. Noninstructional time is ignored, which is permissible only if one assumes that noninstructional time is unimportant, that it is a comparatively minor part of workload, or that the amount of time spent on such activities is highly correlated with the number of credit hours taught. None of these assumptions are tenable (as is discussed in later chapters). They assume further that the same amount of time is involved in teaching all three-credit courses, regardless of the discipline and the course level, an assumption contradicted by data. Thus, although institutional measures are useful for planning and budgeting, they are not useful in studies of workload except as crude estimates or as supplements to other types of measures.

WORKLOAD DATA FROM FACULTY REPORTS

As an alternative to institutional data, researchers can compile data on workload by requesting faculty members to report on their activities using questionnaires, diaries, or work samples. In some studies, faculty are asked to report the amount of time spent in terms of hours per week, in others in terms of percentages. Although the two are interchangeable when one has a measure of the total hours worked per week, each procedure has its arguments for and against.

Percentages are useful for estimating specific activities, hourly estimates for the total work week (Stecklein 1961). Percentages are easier to estimate than are hours, are more meaningful, and make data directly comparable; further, using percentages usually results in less inflated estimates. On the other hand, percentages create problems in estimating costs. Suppose, for example, that two faculty members teach the same course and devote the same number of hours per week to that course. If A works 50 percent more hours per week than B, the percent of time A devotes to the course will be only two-thirds of the percentage reported by B, even though the number of hours is identical (Tyndall and Barnes 1962). While the data are valid, comparing percentages can yield misleading impressions of workload if they are based on different weekly hours.

Thus, hours are usually better than percentages. They are more accurately estimated, are directly comparable between individuals, and can be converted easily to percentages. Hours are used as a standard measure in most industries. They can be directly added to one another without weighting. And they are often referred to in faculty statutes and in collective bargaining agreements that specify the number of hours of teaching, the number of office hours, and in some cases the number of hours per week to be spent on campus.

Sample
In any study of faculty workload, including studies using institutional data, one must first define the population to be studied and then decide whether to study the entire population or only a representative sample of that population. Defining the population involves deciding which types of faculty members should be included or excluded. Should the study include teaching assistants, faculty devoting full

time to sponsored research, department heads, persons devoting a major portion of their time to administrative duties, extension faculty, librarians, faculty in law and medicine? Including "atypical" groups can make standard forms inappropriate and can distort the data. The decision to include or exclude certain types of faculty should be based on the purposes of the survey and the uses to be made of the data. The way that the population is defined will influence the results obtained.

The decision to sample the faculty depends upon the size of the smallest group to be described. To describe a large institution or large segments of an institution, sampling would be appropriate. To characterize small groups, such as departments or ranks within a department, sampling would not be useful.

When samples are appropriate, they have advantages. Because fewer people are involved, samples are less expensive. It is possible to follow up with individual non-responders, and sometimes it is possible to use individual interviews to validate the data. Using a sample that is stratified by field or rank can help ensure that it is representative. But faculty and administration often distrust samples (Romney 1971). Many people disapprove of sampling faculty members because they believe so many cases are atypical that it is impossible to generalize.

A biased sample can result when not everyone responds to the survey questionnaire. If the response rate is significantly less than 100 percent, the validity of the data can be questioned. While some faculty members are interested, respond willingly, and are honest in their replies, others respond unwillingly, if at all, and consciously or unconsciously distort their replies. Thus, one should not assume that those who do not respond are similar to those who do.

Timing
A number of questions about timing have to be decided in any survey of faculty work habits.

Time of administration
A survey can request data concurrently, retrospectively, or prospectively. *Concurrent data collection,* often used, is probably the best method. The data are collected either while the activity is going on (as in work sampling) or soon

thereafter (as in the use of logs or diaries). Problems arising from faulty memory are minimized. Most people can remember what they did during the past 24 or 48 hours, even though they might not be able to remember what they did a week ago. The major problem with the method, however, is that many people view it as a bothersome and time-consuming chore.

Retrospective data collection, which is also often used, usually involves the distribution of a questionnaire at the end of a semester or quarter. Faculty members are requested to estimate how they spent their time during that period. Because faulty memory could seriously distort the data, it is important to obtain the data as soon as possible after an event occurs.

In *prospective data collection,* which is only occasionally used, faculty members are asked at the beginning of a semester to estimate how much time they expect to spend on specific activities during the coming semester. It is assumed that the estimate will be based on past experiences, sharing most of the advantages and disadvantages of retrospective data collection. In addition, the individual who prospectively estimates his expenditures of time might, consciously or unconsciously, conform to those estimates, which could be good or bad.

Two studies dealt explicitly with the relationship between faculty estimates of time spent on various activities and objective measurements of the time spent (Lorents 1971; Ritchey 1959). Both found that estimates were close to actual time in some categories but very different in other categories. The most accurate estimates were of the time spent in classes; the least accurate were of the time spent in personal activity during regular school hours, where the average observed value was more than double the estimate of 7.2 percent (Ritchey 1959). Such data indicate that time reports are sometimes inaccurate, implying that faculty responses should be treated as estimates—possibly overestimates—rather than as accurate indicators of actual time.

Many people disapprove of sampling faculty members because they believe so many cases are atypical that it is impossible to generalize.

Time period covered

The researcher must also decide whether the survey will cover a day, several days, a week, a month, a semester, or a year (all of which have been used in past surveys). To minimize negative reactions from faculty, the time covered by the study should be the shortest period that will yield accurate data. Although many studies have used periods of one or two weeks, assuming that the period was typical, this assumption is questionable because week-by-week activities can vary widely. In one case (Ritchey 1959), data plotted week by week for a full semester indicated that the percentage of total time devoted to teaching ranged from about 36 to 50 percent, with an average of 42 percent, a figure that was not obtained for any single week during the semester! This study vividly documents the impossibility of finding a typical week. Every faculty member is aware of week-to-week variations in specific activities; some weeks seem to involve only committee meetings, others, grading papers. Thus, it is desirable to study a quarter or a semester (Now 1963; Ritchey 1959; Stecklein 1961). Perhaps the best solution is to collect data covering an entire academic year, with separate estimates for each quarter or semester (Stecklein 1961).

Time allocation

Problems of time allocation arise when a faculty member devotes time to an activity that combines several different functions. If a faculty member spends 30 hours per week working in a laboratory during which time she does research relating to a government grant, supervises graduate student assistants, and writes research reports, some of which will be presented in graduate seminars, how should the 30 hours be allocated among the categories of research, administrative supervision, teaching, and preparing for class?

Although these kinds of questions often can be ignored, they became very important after the publication in 1979 of the Office of Management and Budget's Circular A-21. The circular requires faculty members who work on government-sponsored research projects to account for 100 percent of their time, allocating it to one of five categories—which are different from the categories usually used in workload studies—sponsored research, instruction, indirect cost activities, other sponsored activities, or other institutional activities (Thomas 1982).

Allocating time in this fashion can be very time consuming and potentially very disturbing to faculty members who are upset by what they perceive as meaningless record keeping. Several rules could simplify the process: (1) Allocate all of the time involved in administering research and in training and educating research assistants to research; (2) allocate all of the time that a researcher spends in a "research area" to research; (3) when subdividing time is necessary, use a fifty-fifty split (Thomas 1982). Although the suggestions are arbitrary, they do simplify the job and in the long run are probably just as useful as any alternative procedures.

Data Collection Procedures
Workload data can be collected from questionnaires, interviews, diaries, or work samples.

Questionnaires
Questionnaires are used most often to collect data for studies of faculty workload. According to Stecklein (1961), a special form for each institution, rather than a standardized instrument, should be used. The questionnaire should be only three or four pages long, simple, uncomplicated, and uncluttered in appearance, and sufficiently adaptable so that faculty members can report all activities without encountering major problems in categorization. Too much flexibility, however, can lead to problems in coding and analyzing the data (Romney 1971).

A standardized, cross-institutional approach has been developed at NCHEMS (Manning 1974; Manning and Romney 1973; Romney 1971). Although each institution can adapt the questionnaire to its own needs, any changes that are made tend to lessen the comparability of the data.

The cost of questionnaires is comparatively low but varies depending on whether the questionnaires are mailed to faculty members or àre administered in small groups. The latter approach may be preferable, particularly the first time the questionnaire is administered (Manning and Romney 1973).

Interviews
Interviews, which are seldom used, tend to be both expensive and time consuming, but they do have a number of advantages. First, the response rate tends to be high. People may not fill out and return questionnaires, but most faculty members find it difficult to avoid talking to an inter-

viewer, particularly one who has the backing of the university administration. Second, the interviewer can specify exactly what information he wants, and the respondent can clarify ambiguous answers. Interviews are useful for following up and validating the results obtained from questionnaires (Romney 1971).

Diaries

While diaries and time logs have not been used often, they have much to recommend them, particularly the accuracy of the data obtained. When a faculty member keeps a conscientious record of how time is spent, recording activities daily, the resulting data are more accurate than data obtained by questionnaires or interviews. Even if the data are not entered as often as they should be, they will probably be relatively accurate, because the time between the event and its recall is short and because activities must be fit into specific time periods.

The major problems with this technique is faculty members' unwillingness to devote the time and effort required to complete a diary. This negativism is particularly acute if the faculty member is requested to continue the diary over a long period of time. Thus, in one instance when faculty members were requested to complete three one-week diaries covering different periods, about 90 percent of the faculty completed the first diary, 50 percent the second, and 40 percent the third (Balfour 1970). The low rates of return on the third round made those data of questionable accuracy.

Work samples

Work samples have been used widely in industry but seldom used in studying faculty activities. One study in which the technique worked well involved 20 faculty members in one department, each of whom was contacted at random intervals four times a day for a full semester and asked to describe what he was doing at the time. A total of 330 observations were collected on each individual. To determine time use after regular hours, the researcher randomly selected 20 days and required the faculty member to report retrospectively the job-related activities he engaged in (Ritchey 1959). The study demonstrated that the technique was feasible for use in higher education and that it was useful, easy to administer, accurate, inexpensive, and dependent only on faculty members' understanding and cooperation.

In another study, the researcher used an electronic device that had been programmed to "beep" at random intervals. When faculty members heard the beep, they were supposed to record what they were doing at the time, using a predetermined set of categories (Lorents 1971). Each recording was to take about 30 seconds, and the total time per week would not exceed 30 minutes. Respondents preferred work sampling to questionnaires. To be useful, such a technique should sample faculty members eight to 10 times during an eight-hour day for three or four weeks. Despite its seeming excellence, the technique is not widely used, perhaps because researchers consider it too complex.

Workload Categories
The problem of defining categories is basic to any study or discussion of faculty workload. Each category must be precisely defined and specific examples given of the kinds of activities included and excluded.

The number of categories used depends upon the purpose of the study. Although most studies use five to 10 categories, some use many more. One researcher identified 25 components that represent "duties that any faculty member might be expected to perform as part of his faculty workload" (Miller 1968, p. 28). An advantage of using a large number of categories is that they can later be combined into clusters of related activities.

Although the central importance of having an agreed-upon set of standard categories with precise definitions has been emphasized often (Lorents 1971; Manning and Romney 1973; Stecklein 1960), the probability of attaining this goal is low because most institutions prefer their own locally developed idiosyncratic categories. Thus, because standardized categories are not used, the results obtained at different institutions are seldom comparable, and problems may arise in interpreting the data. While increased comparability would result if the categories developed in the faculty activity analysis studies at NCHEMS had been adopted (Manning and Romney 1973; Romney 1971), it has not occurred.

The basic categories used in most studies are instruction, research, professional development, institutional service, advisement/counseling, public service, and personal activities.

Instruction refers to all of the time devoted to teaching, including time spent in class, preparing for class, preparing and grading assignments and examinations, and time spent talking to students about the class (but not time spent advising students).

Research refers to a broad range of intellectual and scholarly activities that normally result in some type of scholarly output. It includes scholarly research, writing books, articles, plays, poems, or reviews, painting, composing music, giving a recital, and so on. It does not include preparing lectures for class or reading that does not result in scholarly output. Some authors—Stecklein, for example—recommend that a distinction be made between sponsored and nonsupported research.

Professional development refers to time spent in activities that contribute to the professional knowledge of a faculty member. It includes reading material related to the profession, attending professional meetings and conventions, taking courses, and engaging in discussions with colleagues. It does not include time spent reading newspapers and magazines, watching television, or engaging in general discussions, even though some faculty members argue that everything they do is job related.

Institutional service refers to a broad category of activities, including general administration (correspondence, serving as department head, keeping records, preparing budgets, etc.), attending meetings and functions common to university campuses, participating in registration, student services, and administrative duties that are part of the assigned workload.

Advisement/counseling, although sometimes included under administrative activities, should be kept separate as many academics consider it a very important, though often neglected, part of the duties of a faculty member.

Public service includes those professional activities that occur outside of the institution—consulting, giving lectures or speeches, holding office in a public organization, and so on. Although they can include holding office in a professional organization or editing a journal, those activities are usually listed as professional development.

Personal activities are seldom included as a category in workload studies, but they should because some time-sampling studies indicate that they account for about 15 percent of the total work time of faculty members (Ritchey 1959). This category includes activities related to personal interests, relaxation, casual conversations, friendly lunches, reading newspapers and magazines, phone calls to family or friends, and so forth. In Ritchey's survey, *every* faculty member who responded underestimated the amount of time spent on personal activities. Thus, such activities account for a significant amount of a faculty member's total time on campus, even though they are not part of a person's workload.

Time versus Effort

The question of whether workload studies should empha-size time or effort dates back to the earliest study by Koos (1919), who stated that although workload is influenced by both the time and fatigue (presumably reflecting effort) involved in faculty activities, data show that fatigue is not important. Nevertheless, researchers periodically stress what particular assignments "take out of" a faculty mem-ber (Now 1963). Some faculty members believe that effort is more important than time, even though "no one has come up with a widely accepted definition of effort other than time" (Stecklein 1974, p. 15).

The emphasis on effort has been criticized: The concept is difficult to understand, different people may interpret it differently, and it is easy to distort estimates of the expen-diture of effort (Stoddart 1973). Because of these limita-tions, measures of effort are appropriate only when it is very clear that the amount of energy expended during dif-ferent units of time varies widely and when periods of highly intense effort necessitate rest or work at a slower pace (Stoddart 1973). Under these conditions, rest time should be included as part of work time; under other condi-tions, measures of effort are not needed.

Faculty Attitudes

Studies of workload require the cooperation of faculty members, department chairs, deans, and departmental secretaries. Faculty members who are willing to cooperate supply accurate data, but if the cooperative attitude is lacking, the return rate will be low and the data of questionable accuracy.

Faculty members dislike and distrust studies of their work habits (Balfour 1970; Eagleton 1977; Huther 1974; Lorents 1971; Warden 1974), and their negative attitudes can be traced to beliefs that quantification results in inaccuracy and distortion (Creswell 1978), that because faculty members are professionals they should not be subject to statistical scrutiny, just as they do not have to punch time clocks (Bunnell 1960), and that the data will be used to harm the faculty (Doi 1961). As a group, they tend to value highly the flexibility of an academic schedule and the amount of freedom it allows. Faculty members often perceive studies of workload as beneficial neither to them personally nor to their unit (Warden 1974). Many faculty members, particularly those in the humanities, believe that the most important aspects of their jobs are qualitative and cannot be quantitatively measured. Faculty with these attitudes tend to be critical of workload studies and consequently may not be honest in their responses.

Thus, every workload study should attempt to induce positive, cooperative attitudes among the faculty. Probably the most important factor is to explain the purposes and uses of the survey to the faculty. The researcher should explain that the data will hurt neither individuals nor departments. A faculty advisory committee to participate in the planning and the execution of the study is desirable (Stecklein 1961). If the faculty is unionized, it is important to get the union to agree to the study. Holding meetings of departments to discuss the study can be helpful in eliciting cooperation, and it is helpful if the request for cooperation comes in a letter from the president rather than from the office of institutional research. Finally, the faculty should be told that they will be informed of the results of the study.

Manning and Romney (1973) postulated four conditions that can increase faculty members' acceptance of workload studies: (1) if faculty members find it difficult to ignore administrative requests for data; (2) if they believe the data will help their department; (3) if they are knowledgeable about the data collection procedures; and (4) if they believe the data were requested by an external government agency. In a later study of these hypotheses, the data supported only the hypothesis that faculty accept studies designed to provide data that will be useful to their department, and the study recommended that administrators try to convince faculty of the departmental benefits that could result from the study (Creswell 1978).

Accuracy of the Data

Accurate data are central to studies of faculty workload. The accuracy of a set of data is determined by obtaining measurements of reliability and validity. In workload studies, *reliability* is the extent to which similar results would be obtained if measurements were taken at different times. Reliability depends on the clarity of the definitions of categories, the length of the time period studied, and the representativeness of the time period studied. While few studies of reliability as such have been undertaken, the consensus of persons familiar with the literature appears to be that most methods yield relatively reliable data unless a short or unrepresentative time period is used.

Validity in faculty workload studies is the degree to which a faculty member's report corresponds to the way in which the time was actually spent. The problem arises from concern about the accuracy of self-reported data. To what extent will a faculty member try to make it appear that he works harder than he actually does? What percentage of faculty members consciously or unconsciously distort their reports? Romney (1971) noted that the validity of data obtained from questionnaires is not always acceptable; it is higher if diaries, interviews, or work samples are used. Thus, when discrepancies appear, data obtained through time sampling should probably be considered most valid, data from a diary would rank second, and data obtained from interviews or questionnaires, both of which require retrospective estimates, would be least valid.

The percentage of faculty who return completed forms is an important influence on the validity of the data. Unless a large percentage of the faculty return their forms, the accuracy of the data is questionable because there is little reason to assume that those who respond have work patterns similar to those who do not respond.

Studies of the validity of faculty workload data are much needed. While many techniques might be used, an adapta-

Faculty members dislike and distrust studies of their work habits.

tion of the method of convergent validity described by Campbell and Fiske (1959) seems most appropriate. Data regarding the workload of faculty members should be obtained by several different methods (diaries, questionnaires, and work samples, for example). Data also should be obtained from several alternative sources, such as the department head, departmental colleagues, and the faculty member's spouse. When data are obtained from both faculty members and department heads, the two estimates often converge; when they do not, department heads might discuss the discrepancy with the faculty member.

Some techniques are less objectionable than others. While a faculty member might resent having another faculty member talk about how he spends his time, he might be willing to discuss his questionnaire results with his department chair (Stecklein 1961). A procedure in which the department head completes the activity forms for every person in the unit and then asks the faculty member to review them might be appropriate (Romney 1971). Either approach increases the validity of the data.

Thus, both in planning and in conducting a study of faculty workload, the researcher must pay careful attention to the accuracy of the data obtained. Accuracy can never be guaranteed, but careful attention should help to maximize the reliability and validity of any data that are obtained.

Individual Differences
It is universally recognized that faculty members constitute a very diverse group of individuals who often behave idiosyncratically. Anyone who has ever attended a faculty meeting can testify to the wide range of opinions, attitudes, and personalities exhibited.

Although individual differences are usually ignored in studies of workload, some researchers have cited data documenting them. The following ranges have been reported:

- From 4.0 to 14.9 hours per day, with an average of 8.5 hours per day (Koos 1919);
- From 2 to 107 hours per week, with a median of 58 hours per week (Charters 1942);
- An average of 58.3 hours per week with a standard deviation of 10.6 hours (Thompson 1971);

- An average of 55 hours per week, with a standard deviation of 12.5 hours (Yuker 1974).

Assuming a normal, bell-shaped distribution, this information would imply that two out of three faculty members work 42 to 68 hours per week and that 95 percent of all faculty work between 30 and 80 hours per week. Whatever the true figures are, they clearly vary widely.

These studies all assume a normal distribution with work times symmetrically distributed around the average value. An alternative assumption is that faculty members' workload patterns are skewed rather than symmetrical. Discussions among faculty indicate that they perceive a great deal of variation, often being able to cite one colleague who works a maximum of 15 hours per week and another who works a minimum of 60 hours. A recent article pointed out that positively skewed data are found in many fields and depict phenomena in which a low level of performance is quite frequent and a high level of performance rare (Walberg et al. 1984). Under such conditions, most of the productivity comes from a small percentage of the population. The many examples cited in the article contain several items pertinent to faculty workload—for example, publications, citations, and income—indicating that skewed distributions may accurately describe faculty activity and productivity.

INSTRUCTIONAL ACTIVITIES

Instructional time refers to all time spent on activities directly related to teaching; it includes time spent in class, preparing for class, preparing tests and assignments, grading tests and assignments, and other similar activities. To measure instructional time, one could estimate the total time devoted to all activities related to instruction, or one could break the estimate into components, a procedure that has several advantages. Information about components facilitates comparisons that elucidate the teaching process and the interrelationship of the factors involved. For example, it would be valuable to obtain data relating the amount of time teachers spend preparing for class to teaching effectiveness. And estimates based on components are probably more reliable.

Time spent in class usually includes all time spent in the classroom during regularly scheduled hours as well as time spent in scheduled individual study courses and thesis advisement. Sometimes the activities related to individual study are separated. Class time is generally defined in terms of hours per week, and it often corresponds to the number of assigned hours of credit in the instructor's teaching load. Contact hours tend to be a better measure than credit hours.

Some studies distinguish between time spent in teaching and time spent in "formal instruction" (Ladd and Lipset 1977, for example). Ladd and Lipset's data indicate that faculty responses to the two questions correspond about 80 percent of the time. In the other cases, hours devoted to formal instruction tend to be lower. Thus, the wording of the question is important.

Preparation time refers to time spent in preparing lectures, demonstrations, laboratory experiments, course outlines, and reading lists, setting up laboratories or studios, and supervising course assistants. The Ladd and Lipset (1977) data indicate the following relationships.

Class Hours	Mean Preparation Hours
1–4	5.5
5–8	10.8
9–16	12.5
17–34	9.1

Thus, the data appear to indicate a complex inverse U curve relationship between total preparation time and teaching time, with the most time spent by those who teach nine to 16 hours. Persons who teach five or more hours per week spend nine to 12.5 hours preparing for class, regardless of the number of hours spent in class. Increasing course load beyond 12 hours seems not to lead to increased time spent in preparation.

The same study yielded data indicating a relationship between the amount of time spent preparing for class and the faculty member's expressed interest in research or teaching. Persons very much interested in research (who tend to teach fewer hours) spent the least time (12.4 hours); those interested in both but leaning toward research spent 18.2 hours. Faculty members interested in both but leaning toward teaching spent the most time (22.9 hours), slightly more than those heavily interested in teaching, who averaged 20.6 hours preparing for class.

Evaluation time refers to time spent preparing and grading quizzes, tests, examinations, homework assignments, term papers, and other written work, as well as time spent writing evaluations of students. Although this category may not always be easy to separate from preparation, the distinction can be useful.

Little is known about the relative amounts of time devoted to preparation and evaluation compared to time spent in class. "The traditional idea that two hours outside the classroom are spent for each hour of classroom instruction has a most uncertain ancestry, and appears to be especially open to question when it is taken as a standard for nearly all faculty, regardless of rank and levels and subjects taught" (Stecklein 1961, p. 4). (Some data relating to this question are presented in the chapter describing total workload.)

Instructional time also can be categorized by distinguishing between group instruction and individual instruction (Lorents 1971), which might be useful for general institutional purposes, because different scales of remuneration might be applied for those types of activities.

Classroom instruction refers to the type of traditional teaching that accounts for most of the assigned teaching load of most faculty members at most institutions. Grouped together in this category are lecture courses, sem-

inars, and laboratory sections that meet at regularly scheduled hours and involve interaction between a teacher and a
group of students. It is usually measured in terms of an
assigned number of semester hours or quarter hours of
teaching.

Individual instruction includes readings courses, independent study courses, research courses, honors courses,
tutorials, and supervision of theses and dissertations, as
well as serving on committees that evaluate or supervise a
written report like a master's essay or doctoral dissertation. Although this type of activity could in theory be measured by recording the total number of hours per week
devoted to it, the actual measurement is usually not that
simple because a tenuous relationship usually exists
between the number of credits and the amount of work
performed by the teacher or the student. Often the weekly
"schedule" of meetings is irregular. Instead, the workload
has peaks and valleys, with several hours of time being
required in some weeks and no hours in other weeks.
Because one-to-one instruction is costly, it is important to
obtain accurate time estimates so that the institution can
measure its cost relative to the cost of group instruction.

These complexities indicate that it is impossible to specify the relationship between the number of contact hours
and total instructional time or total workload. Even so,
several people have devised arbitrary formulas. Hauck
(1969) set up a formula that assigns 1.53 hours per week in
preparation time for each hour spent in class and 0.1 hour
per week for each student and each class hour, claiming
that this formula results in total out-of-class time that is
usually double the number of hours spent in class. Simmons (1970), on the other hand, allotted three times the
total number of contact hours as preparation time for each
nonrepetitive course taught, "based on the assumption that
an adequate job of instruction cannot be done with less
effort" (Simmons 1970, p. 34). All such attempts to arbi-
trarily assign standardized numbers to represent the ratio
of total instructional time to contact hours should be
rejected, however, because all of the data indicate that the
relationship is complex and is mediated by other factors.

"Special assignments" refers to all instructional duties
other than regular classroom teaching. They can include
curriculum development, supervision of dissertations and

student teachers, and teaching in competency-based programs. Because these assignments usually involve several hours of "released time" from regular teaching duties, they have to be defined in terms of equivalent semester hours.

Curriculum development is seldom included as a component of workload, although provision may be made for preparation of new courses. Sometimes departments set up a curriculum committee and give each member some released time.

Supervision of dissertations is treated differently at different institutions. Some universities, usually those with extensive graduate programs and low teaching loads, expect each faculty member to handle a specified number of graduate students as part of his or her regular teaching load. Other universities define supervision of dissertations in terms of equivalent credit hours, and faculty members are given released time or extra compensation.

Little research has been done of the subject, except for an excellent study by Blackburn and Trowbridge (1973), who sent questionnaires to faculty members in six departments at a large midwestern university. The faculty respondents reported they devoted an average (median) of 13 percent of their time to supervising dissertations. Variation occurred among disciplines, with averages of 7.8 percent in humanities and 17.6 percent in natural sciences. Faculty members expressed the opinion that at any given time a person could serve as chairman of five committees and member of five other committees. Large differences occurred among individuals: Half of the faculty produced all of the Ph.D.s, and some faculty members produced 50 times more than others. The large producers received more grants and more research funds, even though they did not devote more time to research. They spent more time in informal and social contacts with graduate students. The productivity in supervising dissertations was unrelated to age, rank, or teaching effectiveness. Producing one doctorate was equivalent to 33 percent of the workload of the dissertation chairman and 20 percent of the workload of the faculty members with the most productivity (Blackburn and Trowbridge 1973).

In one study of the *supervision of student teachers,* data indicated that the number of student teachers supervised by directors of student teaching ranged from four to 28, with a mean of 11.5 (Solliday 1982). Approximately two out of three supervised fewer than 10 students per term and made an average of five classroom visits per student per year (the range was one to 16).

Competency-based programs involve types of work different from regular programs and consequently require different workload assignments. Faculty members in such programs spend most of their time evaluating students' learning, much time in advising students, and the least time teaching courses (Meeth 1974). Faculty members devote about 33 percent of their time to curriculum development during the first year and 20 to 25 percent in the second year, but the amount varies among disciplines (Feasley 1978).

Time Devoted to Instruction

The total number of hours per week that faculty members devote to instructional activities varies widely. Some "research professors" devote 100 percent of their time to research, while others devote almost all of their time to teaching by minimizing other activities. More generally, however, the amount of time devoted to teaching tends to vary from a low of about 40 percent (Lorents 1971; Orlans 1962; Ritchey 1959; Wilson 1942) to a high of about 70 percent (Bayer 1973; Parsons and Platt 1969; Stickler 1960).

The amount of time devoted to instructional activities is, to a large extent, related to the course load assigned to the faculty member, which may vary from zero to the low twenties in a given semester. In the United States, course loads tend to vary between six and 15 credits.

The amount of time devoted to ancillary instructional activities, such as preparation and evaluation, also varies. Some guidelines suggest that faculty members should devote two hours to ancillary activities for each (50-minute) hour spent in class (Holliman 1977; Institute for Research 1978). If a person teaches 12 hours per week and spends 24 hours in related activities, it would constitute 65 percent of a 55-hour week. Estimates of the total time devoted to instructional activities range from 43 percent (Institute for Research 1978) to 50 percent (Blackburn and Trowbridge 1973) to 59 percent for faculty at four-year institutions and 80 percent for those at community colleges (Stecklein, Willie, and Lorenz 1983). In one study (Ladd and Lipset 1977), data indicate that percents range between

33 and 50, which makes estimates of 4½ outside hours for each hour in class (Campbell 1982) unbelievable.

Workload data indicate that teaching loads are related to demographic factors (country, institution, discipline), scheduling factors (class size, course level, course type, preparations), and individual factors (rank, gender, individual differences).

Country

Data obtained from 80 universities in 50 countries indicate that most teaching loads vary from seven to 12.5 hours per week, although some are as high as 23 (Onushkin 1972). In general, the highest teaching loads are found in developing countries in Asia, Latin America, and Central America. Workloads at institutions in African countries range in the middle. The lowest teaching loads are in European countries, with the United States and Canada second. In countries that have several types of institutions of higher education, loads vary by institutional type.

While teaching loads vary by country, the differences are not as great as expected. Teaching loads tend to be similar in countries at similar stages of development. Factors such as type of institution, discipline, and faculty rank tend to influence teaching loads in similar ways in most countries.

Type of Institution

Teaching loads tend to be different at two-year colleges, four-year colleges, and universities, and at high-quality and low-quality institutions. They also tend to be different at black and religious colleges compared to other similar institutions (Billingsley 1982).

Teaching loads are lower at high-quality institutions than at lower-quality institutions (Baldridge et al. 1978; Fulton and Trow 1974; Parsons and Platt 1969; Stecklein, Willie, and Lorenz 1983; Wilson 1942). Although definitions vary, "high-quality institutions" tend to offer doctorates and to have more resources, which enable them to earmark funds for faculty research and other activities that result in lower teaching loads. They also tend to hire faculty members who are more interested in research than in teaching. For example, only 15 percent of the faculty members at high-quality research institutions said that they were very heavily interested in teaching, compared to 77 percent of junior college faculty (Fulton and Trow 1974).

Discipline

Differences in workload among disciplines are complex. On the one hand, teaching load schedules at a given institution tend to be relatively uniform except for some of the professional schools, such as medicine or law. On the other hand, the amount of time required for preparation and evaluation varies widely among disciplines (Stickler 1960).

Perhaps the reason for this variation is that a single academic profession does not exist; instead, it encompasses many professions, one for each discipline, which has its own history, intellectual style, preferences for types of research and publication, and even different career lines (Light 1974). Some disciplines, such as psychology, could even be divided into subdisciplines because conceptual orientation and work habits differ greatly—in this case among clinical, experimental, and social psychologists. Similarly, psychology is usually classified as one of the social sciences, even though some department members think and behave like humanities faculty while others think and behave like scientists.

Although most institutions group disciplines in similar ways (for example, humanities, sciences, social sciences, education, business, law, medicine), social science researchers have attempted to devise alternative groupings. One such classification categorized each discipline in a university as *hard* or *soft,* reflecting the extent to which the discipline used a paradigm reflecting consensus with regard to the problems to be studied and the methods to be used; *pure* or *applied,* and *life* or *nonlife* (Biglan 1973a, 1973b). Faculty members' commitment to teaching, research, or service activities varied according to discipline. Faculty members in "soft" areas preferred teaching and spent more time teaching, while those in "hard" areas preferred research and devoted more time to it. Scholars in the "pure" areas liked research more than those in "applied" areas but did not spend more time at it. Persons in applied areas preferred service activities and devoted more time to them. Faculty in the "life" areas liked teaching less than those in "nonlife" areas and devoted less

The amount of time required for preparation and evaluation varies widely among disciplines.

time to it. Scholars working in the hard disciplines produce fewer books and monographs but more journal articles, while persons in the applied areas tend to produce technical reports.

Others have used these categories in studies of workload. (Interestingly, the rate of response to questionnaires also differs, which could influence the reliability of the data obtained in workload studies.) Faculty members in the soft-pure-nonlife category (humanities) devoted the most time to teaching (52 percent), while those in the hard-pure-life (biology) and hard-applied life (agriculture) categories devoted the least time to teaching, 27 percent and 20 percent, respectively (Smart and McLaughlin 1978). SCH/FTE was higher in the soft than in the hard disciplines, higher in the pure than in the applied areas, and higher in the nonlife than in the life disciplines (Muffo and Langston 1981). Interestingly, in all cases except pure versus applied, the disciplines with higher SCH/FTE ratios also had higher salaries. On the other hand, at seven large public institutions, while some departmental ratios were similar at all institutions, others showed very wide interinstitutional percentile ranges: biology 8 to 95, business 20 to 100, French 34 to 100, history 24 to 100, English 33 to 84, law 45 to 97 (Jedamus 1974). One should therefore exercise caution in making generalizations.

Hesseldenz (1976) used a different set of categories (developed by Holland (1973)) based on the abilities individuals believe they have, the tasks they enjoy doing, and what their values are. Departments were classified as realistic, investigative, social, enterprising, or artistic. While these categorizations may be intuitively meaningful, they are quite different from the way most institutions of higher education are organized and from Biglan's categories. Nevertheless, the percentage of time devoted to instruction by faculty in different departments was clearly different: artistic 64 percent, social 54 percent, enterprising 51 percent, investigative 47 percent, and realistic 43 percent.

Thus, workload differs among disciplines. In addition, some academic disciplines have special needs or requirements. Teaching loads at law schools, for example, are specified in the bylaws of the Association of American Law Schools—eight or 10 class hours per week, depending on how repetitive classes are counted. Some institutions adjust the assigned course loads of faculty members in departments of English (Snepp 1968). Many adjust the assignments for laboratory courses and physical education courses.

Class Size

Although many have offered the opinion that larger classes require extra time, a person who teaches 600 students does not work 60 times as hard as one teaching 10 students; in fact, he may work less because he has assistance in grading papers and in other tasks (Caplow 1960). Talking to 200 students is quite different from talking to 25 students, however (Bailey 1968), and this opinion appears to be more popular. All 75 institutions in one survey agreed that large classes require more time (Sexson 1967). Some institutions assign extra workload credits to faculty members who teach large classes (Shulman 1980).

Contrary to popular opinion, however, most researchers report that any effect of class size is minor. Thus, when Reeves et al. (1933) correlated class size with a faculty member's estimates of the time and energy required by a course, they obtained a coefficient of correlation equal to $+.18$, $\pm.03$, and concluded that teaching load is not significantly influenced by class size. The lack of evidence of a relationship between class size and time devoted to teaching has had little influence on faculty workload formulas, many of which assign arbitrary weights to different class sizes (for example, Hauck 1969; Howell 1962; Miller 1968; Sexson 1967).

Because the data indicate a negligible influence of class size on workload and because data indicate no relationship between class size and student learning (Laughlin 1976; Yuker 1974), it is more important to examine the variables that mediate the effects of class size than try to generalize about its effects. Data pertaining to the following variables are needed:

1. The amount of time spent in class, which is independent of class size. The amount of effort or energy expended during that time may vary, but effort cannot be adequately defined or measured.
2. The amount of time spent preparing for class, which might vary as a result of class size.

---

3. The amount of time spent grading papers, which might vary with class size. The relationship, however, could be negative or positive. Graduate assistants and multiple choice exams could significantly decrease grading time. It would be more meaningful to consider the number and types of written assignments and who grades them rather than class size per se.
4. The effect of class size on the amount of time spent interacting with students, which is difficult to predict. The most important influence is probably the instructor's personality and attitude. Students' perceptions are also important; students in large classes might be less likely to try to see the instructor or might interact more readily with teaching assistants.

Several conclusions concerning class size can be drawn. Despite its use in workload formulas and despite the popular belief that class size is an important determinant of workload, it is not important. The emphasis given to class size is an empirical question that ideally should be determined separately for each course and each teacher and based on the number of hours devoted to preparation and grading, not inferred from arbitrary formulas.

Course Level

It is often assumed that upper-division courses are more difficult to teach than lower-division courses and that graduate courses require the most time and effort. Some institutions explicitly take this assumption into account by giving instructors who teach graduate courses reduced teaching loads. One study of 46 universities revealed that 22 percent reduced loads for graduate teaching, 65 percent did not differentiate between graduate and undergraduate courses, and 13 percent made other distinctions (Hanesian 1977). In another study, course preparation and administration time did not vary as a function of course level (Maryland Council 1975).

"Conflicting conclusions characterize studies regarding the effects of level of instruction on faculty load" (Stickler 1960, p. 88). Some investigators (Kelly 1926 and Koos 1919, for example) concluded that course level is an important factor; others (Reeves et al. 1933) present data indicating that the amount of time and effort devoted to a course steadily decreases as one increases the course level. The conflict is also reflected in workload formulas, some of which weight all courses equally, regardless of level, others of which give graduate courses four times as much weight as undergraduate courses (Hill 1969). Assumptions not based on data can be deadly!

These discrepancies in data and opinions result, at least in part, from differences in subject matter and differences in the teaching styles of individual professors. Thus, one can conclude that while other aspects of courses may be important, course level, like class size, should not be considered a major influence on faculty workload.

Course Type
Although course type would be assumed to exert an important influence on preparation time, few data support that assumption and additional research is needed. The major data come from the 65-year-old study by Koos (1919), who calculated ratios to indicate the total number of hours required to prepare and present a one-hour class. His ratios ranged from a low of 1.17 for field work (that is, one hour of field work and .17 hour of preparation time) to a high of 2.98 for a lecture (that is, 1.98 hours of preparation), close to the hypothetical two-to-one ratio.

Most institutions ignore mode of presentation. All one-hour classes are considered equivalent, whether they involve student recitations, seminars, discussions, or lectures. One distinction made in the past was that two laboratory hours were considered the equivalent of one teaching hour (Kelly 1926), but this ratio has been changed at many schools, where laboratory hours are now considered equal to teaching hours.

Preparations
It is generally assumed that number of preparations is an important aspect of teaching load. It should take less time to prepare for several sections of the same course than to prepare for an equal number of sections of different courses, an assumption manifest in many workload formulas.

Nevertheless, the data fail to support the commonly accepted assumption. In one study, data indicated few consistent differences based on number of preparations (Koos 1919), and another indicated that a second section of a course requires approximately the same amount of time to prepare and teach as the initial section (Reeves et al. 1933).

Even though the number of preparations may not be an important influence on faculty workload, it seems reasonable to assume that the first time a person teaches a course, more time will be required, and although the research data are limited, they tend to support the assumption. In one study, the time required for the first preparation of a lecture was 70 percent higher than for subsequent ones, a seminar was 60 percent higher, mixed lecture and discussion 33 percent, recitation 11 percent, and laboratory 9 percent higher (Koos 1919). Some institutions recognize this factor by reducing the loads of faculty preparing a new course.

Data comparing presentations subsequent to the first are not available. While one might assume that the second and possibly the third preparation also require additional time, a leveling-off point is probably reached relatively quickly. One study reported that no relationship existed between the number of years of teaching experience and the time spent in preparation (McMullen 1927). And the finding that no differences existed between ranks in the time devoted to course preparation is pertinent if one assumes that rank is highly correlated with the amount of teaching experience (Koos 1919).

In this case, data and theory coincide. Even though the data are limited, they indicate that new preparations and extensive revisions of old courses take more time than preparation of courses that have been repeatedly taught. This factor should be considered in describing faculty load.

Rank
Most studies of the relationship between rank and teaching load report an inverse relationship; professors tend to have the lowest teaching loads, assistant professors and instructors the highest. In Maryland, the average load is 8.8 for professors, 10.6 for instructors (Maryland Council 1975); nationally, the average load is 8.4 for professors, 14.3 for instructors (Ladd and Lipset 1977).

With regard to time devoted to instruction, one study reported that full professors devoted 27.1 hours per week to instruction, compared to 33.4 for associate professors and 37.2 for lecturers (University of Connecticut 1976);

another reported that professors devote 46 percent of their time to teaching, assistant professors 56 percent (Hesseldenz 1976). Some data indicate that professors spend 9.4 hours preparing for class, instructors 11.0 (Ladd and Lipset 1977). Finally, instructors are more interested in teaching than in research; in one study, 86 percent said they were heavily interested in teaching or interested in both but leaning toward teaching, compared to 61 percent of the full professors (Ladd and Lipset 1977).

This inverse relationship also exists outside of the United States. In Great Britain, professors devote the least time to teaching, readers and senior lecturers (roughly equivalent to associate professors) are in the middle, and lecturers (assistant professors) spend the most time teaching (Carter 1974). A survey of 80 universities in 50 countries indicated that senior-level faculty teach an average of 8.3 hours per week, middle level 10.8, and junior level 11.9 (Onushkin 1972). The average differences among ranks were much greater in developing countries (senior 8.7 versus junior 12.8) than in developed countries (senior 6.9 versus 8.9) (Onushkin 1972).

Gender
Only recently has the relationship between gender and workload been studied, and that study indicates that no significant differences exist between the workloads of female and male nontenured assistant professors (McLaughlin, Mahan, and Montgomery 1983). Gender differences are small in comparison with the differences attributable to discipline and college. Future studies should include this variable.

Individual Differences
The total time devoted to instruction by individual faculty members who have similar teaching load assignments differs greatly. For example, at the University of Chicago, 9 percent of the faculty devoted 71 percent or more of their time to teaching, 58 percent devoted between 31 percent and 70 percent, and 33 percent devoted 30 percent or less of their time to teaching (Reeves et al. 1933).

People who are interested in teaching tend to be employed at lower-quality institutions, such as junior colleges and four-year colleges (Fulton and Trow 1974). Only

15 percent of the faculty members at high-quality institutions state that their interests lie heavily in teaching, compared to 77 percent in junior colleges. An inverse relationship exists between the time devoted to teaching and the total time devoted to academic pursuits (Myers and Mager 1980). Faculty members who said they work fewer than 40 hours per week reported that they devote 43 percent of their time to teaching, while those who said they work more than 70 hours per week devote 22 percent to teaching; the under-40 group devotes 17 hours to instruction, the 70-plus group 15.5 hours. Apparently, faculty members who put in many hours per week devote the extra time to activities other than teaching!

The amount of time devoted to instructional activities follows a normal rather than a bimodal distribution and consequently cannot be the result of "a large group of overworked faculty counterbalancing another large group of 'shirkers' " (Institute for Research 1978, p. 80). Nonetheless, very large individual differences exist; in a two-day period, one faculty member devoted one-half hour to instruction while another devoted 26 hours.

Differences in faculty members' interest in teaching are reflected in the relative emphasis on teaching at the institutions where persons seek and accept faculty positions and in workload assignments. Perhaps most important, however, the number of hours per week devoted to instructional activities primarily reflects a faculty member's interests rather than the assigned course load. If a faculty member is assigned fewer courses, the total weekly hours devoted to instruction will probably not change; he or she simply spends more time on each course. Similarly, if the teaching load is increased, a faculty member will most probably devote less time to each course.

Consequences of Instructional Load
Although important questions have been raised about the effects of instructional workload on the quality of teaching and of learning, data relating to these questions are almost completely nonexistent. While some faculty members maintain that teaching loads are too high and reduced loads would result in better teaching, this assertion has not been documented. In view of the data indicating wide variations in the amount of time devoted to instruction by faculty

members with similar teaching loads, the most reasonable
assumption is that the quality of both faculty members'
and students' performance is more closely correlated with
the amount of time devoted to instruction than with
teaching load.

RESEARCH, SCHOLARSHIP, AND CREATIVE ACTIVITIES

Most studies of workload contain a category that includes all intellectual activities engaged in by faculty members that distinguish the scholar from the nonscholar. If these activities are overly stressed at an institution, a "publish or perish" attitude results. If they are not sufficiently stressed, the academic reputation of the institution suffers.

This category includes all scholarly activities that have as their goal a specific scholarly production—writing books, articles, or reviews, painting, giving a recital, composing music, reviewing the work of a colleague, or conducting scholarly research. Professional development activities, such as reading and studying or attending workshops or professional meetings, or engaging in other activities that lead to personal intellectual growth but do not lead to specific scholarly output, are excluded from this category.

The term "research" is used in this monograph to cover all of the activities specified in the comprehensive list contained in the *University of California* report:

- creating new knowledge by scientific experimentation;
- painting, creating dramatic or musical compositions;
- conducting field research;
- writing or publishing articles and books;
- supervising research staff;
- developing grant proposals or applications for funding;
- rehearsing for one's music, drama, or dance performance;
- practicing athletics (for physical education faculty);
- reading journals and other literature, viewing art, and attending concerts, only when they bear directly on research or creative activities;
- discussing research with colleagues (Institute for Research 1978).

Research and Teaching
Many pages in the literature of higher education have been devoted to discussions of whether teaching or research is more important at a given type of institution, how much weight should be given to each factor in evaluating faculty members for promotion or tenure, and whether a negative relationship exists between the amount of research performed and teaching performance.

According to Light (1974), research[1] rather than teaching best represents the major mission of institutions of higher education, and scholarly activities and teaching undergraduates are in constant conflict. (Teaching graduate students is more acceptable because it is closer to research at the leading institutions in the United States.) Nevertheless, a surprising percentage of faculty at "lesser universities and colleges" publish papers and books. Using Light's definition of scholarly professionals as those individuals whose core activity is the advancement of knowledge, only the 20 percent of U.S. faculty who publish (Fulton and Trow 1974) would be so defined.

The assumption that teaching and research are negatively related is tenable only if the total time devoted to the two activities remains constant, which is often not the case. It is probable that if teaching loads were reduced, faculty members would either devote more time to activities other than research or reduce their total work week.

Although the question of the relationship between the number of hours devoted to teaching and the number devoted to research is an empirical one, few empirical studies have been completed. One of the best correlated the time devoted to teaching and to research and found that all of the correlation values were small and negative, ranging from $-.02$ to $-.10$ (Koos 1919). Thus, the relationship between teaching time and research time is negligible, and universities should not reduce teaching loads in the hope that it will result in more research. It would be more economical and practical to reduce the teaching schedules of individual instructors who have demonstrated their inclination toward and ability in research. A more recent study concluded that changes in teaching load do not influence research or public service activities unless the teaching load is greatly increased (Hesseldenz 1976). The data appear conclusive: Universities should look for evidence of research productivity rather than assuming that a reduction in teaching load will automatically result in more research.

---

1. Light prefers the term "scholarship" to "research" as data show that academic rewards and professional reputation are based on professional publications rather than research (or teaching), and some important papers are written without research.

Few studies have been performed of individual differences or of the personality variables that correlate with the amount of time devoted to research in an academic setting. One study indicates a strong positive relationship between time spent doing research and expressed interest in research (Ladd and Lipset 1977). Persons who say their interests are heavily in research devote an average of more than 22 hours per week to research, while those whose interests are heavily in teaching devote less than one hour per week, on average (median), to research. Conversely, faculty members heavily interested in research average 5.6 teaching hours per week compared to 12.3 hours for those heavily interested in teaching.

Research Output
Research output can be measured by number of productions (publications, paintings, musical compositions, and so on), quality of productions (number of citations or references, quality of reviews), and less directly by the number and worth of grants received. The several measures tend to be highly intercorrelated so that the result is what Paul Lazarsfeld referred to as an "interchangeability of indices."

Most faculty members produce few or no scholarly works.

Most faculty members produce few or no scholarly works. Of the faculty at institutions of higher education in Minnesota, 85 percent reported that they had produced no creative works during the five-year period 1975 to 1980 (Stecklein, Willie, and Lorenz 1983). In a national sample of 4,383 faculty members, 24 percent had *never* published an article or a book (Ladd 1979). At the other extreme, 2.5 percent had published a total of five or more books plus 21 or more articles, and 1 percent had published more than 10 books plus more than 50 articles. Scholarly productivity tends to be rewarded financially as well as by enhanced reputation and recognition from colleagues. Faculty salaries are influenced more by research than by teaching (Katz 1973; Siegfried and White 1973), and a moderate relationship exists between scholarly productivity and salary increases, with a smaller relationship between teaching effectiveness and salary increases (Hoyt 1974). No relationship is apparent, however, between scholarly publications and teaching effectiveness. When faculty members at Stanford were asked to indicate which factors influence the "flexible" reward system at the university, 78 percent said research, 20 percent teaching, 8 percent university service, and 3 percent external service. When they were asked which factors *should* be influential, 67 percent said research and 51 percent teaching. Thus, even at a major research university, over half of the faculty members believe that teaching performance should influence salaries. Nevertheless, research is "the means by which prestige is usually, and promotion almost always, gained" (Fulton and Trow 1974, p. 31).

Institutional Differences
Many studies have documented institutional differences in both faculty members' interest in research and in research productivity. These differences are positively correlated with ratings of the quality of an institution. In an early study, faculty members at state universities, land grant institutions, and private nondenominational institutions spent substantially more time in research than those who worked at teachers colleges and junior colleges (Evenden, Gamble, and Blue 1933). Thirty-five percent of the faculty at 12 liberal arts colleges devoted no time to research, compared to only 10 percent at universities that receive substantial federal research support (Orlans 1962).

Almost three times as much time was devoted to research in high-quality institutions (35 percent) as in low-quality institutions (12.5 percent) (Parsons and Platt 1969). Further, almost all faculty members said they would have liked to devote more time to research (the ideal time was 45 percent in high-quality and 25 percent in low-quality institutions). At community colleges, 93 percent of the faculty spend less than 10 percent of their time on research, compared to 54 percent at four-year institutions and 27 percent at the University of Minnesota (Stecklein, Willie, and Lorenz 1983). Faculty at doctoral-granting institutions devote 50 to 100 percent more time in research and graduate training than do faculty in other institutions (Baldridge et al. 1978).

Differences in productivity reflect research interest. In the 1970s, several investigators asked faculty members whether their interests lie "heavily in research; in both, leaning toward research; in both, leaning toward teaching; or heavily in teaching" (Behymer and Blackburn 1975; Fulton and Trow 1974; Ladd and Lipset 1975, 1977). Of the faculty at high-prestige universities, 50 percent were either highly interested in research or interested in both research and teaching but leaning toward research, compared to 26 percent at high-prestige four-year institutions and 5 percent at two-year institutions (Fulton and Trow 1974). Similarly, 61 percent of the faculty at high-quality universities expressed research interests, compared to 14 percent at small teacher-oriented colleges (Behymer and Blackburn 1975). At high-prestige universities, 79 percent of the faculty said they currently were engaged in research, compared to 54 percent at prestigious four-year institutions and 14 percent at two-year colleges (Fulton and Trow 1974).

Discipline
Faculty members in the natural sciences devote more time to research than those in mathematics or engineering (Foley 1929). At institutions that receive research support from the federal government, faculty members in the sciences spend about twice as much time on research activities as those in the humanities (Orlans 1962). Those in the social sciences devote almost as much time as those in the sciences.

In the study by Fulton and Trow (1974), the percent of faculty who said they were currently not engaged in any research ranged from a low of 5 percent in biology to a high of 31 percent in the fine arts. Similarly, the percent who said they had no current publications ranged from a low of 16 percent in biology to a high of 56 percent in the fine arts. The percent with current publications, by discipline, included 84 percent in biology, 75 percent in social sciences, 74 percent in physical sciences, 71 percent in engineering, 62 percent in business, 60 percent in education, 59 percent in humanities, and 44 percent in fine arts. Those percentages are supported by other studies: Substantially similar data were reported by the University of Connecticut (1976), except that humanities and fine arts ranked between the physical sciences and engineering, and social work was at the bottom of the list. Thus, the data indicate that the sciences and social sciences have the highest productivity, business, education, and humanities are in the middle, and fine arts are low. These data, however, are influenced by the type of productivity—for example, books versus articles versus paintings.

Differences also exist among disciplines with regard to publication outlets. Research in the "hard" disciplines, such as the sciences and some of the social sciences (psychology, for example), is published in articles rather than in books (Behymer and Blackburn 1975; Creswell and Bean 1981).

In some disciplines—nursing, for example—concern has been expressed about the dearth of faculty research, which may result from the lack of research skills and research socialization during education (Fawcett 1979). Nonresearchers often blame lack of time, even though data indicate that providing time for research seldom results in increased research productivity. Time for research appears to be directly related to the priority assigned to research compared to the priority assigned to teaching, service, and leisure (Fawcett 1979). Research can be done on weekends and during semester breaks, summer vacations, and sabbatical leaves. People who want to do research find time to do it. People who are highly motivated to publish manage to do so.

Rank

Higher-ranked faculty are more productive than those in lower ranks. At the better colleges and universities, 31 percent of the instructors, 66 percent of the assistant professors, 74 percent of the associate professors, and 82 percent of the full professors reported current publications (Fulton and Trow 1974). In another study, 2 percent of the instructors, 13 percent of the assistant professors, 21 percent of the associate professors, and 29 percent of the full professors had published five or more articles in the previous two years (Behymer and Blackburn 1975). And other data reveal that instructors say they spend 11 hours per week on research, assistant professors 12, associate professors 14, and full professors 15 (University of Connecticut 1976). While these differences appear small, four hours a week represents 200 hours a year, which can result in differences in research output.

But others found no differences in rank; faculty spend about 25 percent of their time on research activities, regardless of rank (Hesseldenz 1976). With increasing age and increasing rank, some professors spend less time on research and more on administration, and others continue to spend large portions of their time on research and publication (Allison and Stewart 1974). Perhaps the differences between the two groups can be accounted for by the "Matthew effect" (Merton 1968) or by the related concept of cumulative advantage: Highly productive scientists who receive positive feedback through recognition and resources tend to maintain or even increase their productivity with increasing age, while those who produce little early in their careers tend to produce even less later.

Gender

Most data indicate that men publish more than women, perhaps because female faculty members have many of the characteristics associated with low productivity: holding degrees from and appointments at less prestigious schools, teaching humanities rather than science, teaching undergraduate courses, holding lower rank, and being less interested in research (Behymer and Blackburn 1975). Some of these differences can stem from discrimination; others may reflect differences in socialization. The important finding is that when these variables are parceled out, gender differences disappear. Women who have the characteristics associated with high research productivity are just as productive as men (Clemente 1973; Over 1982).

Individual Differences

Although variables such as institution, discipline, rank, and gender are related to research productivity, they do not account for all of the variance. Two professors in the same discipline at the same institution, of the same sex and similar rank, might have quite different records of productivity. And a female associate professor of English at a middle-level, four-year college might be many times more productive than a male full professor of biology at a major research university. These differences can probably be attributed to a combination of individual factors, including interest and the types and amounts of feedback received.

A positive relationship exists between the percent of time devoted to research and the total number of hours worked per week (Myers and Mager 1980). People who work fewer than 40 hours per week spend about 8 percent of that time (three hours) in research. Those who work 60 to 69 hours per week devote 15 percent of their time (at least nine hours) to research. Apparently, spending more time working permits individuals interested in research to devote more time to it.

A high interest in research is the best predictor of research productivity, and frequent communication with colleagues at other institutions is second best (Behymer and Blackburn 1975). In addition, productive researchers subscribe to more journals: 4 percent of the faculty receive no journals, 28 percent receive one or two, 35 percent three or four, 26 percent five to 10, and 4 percent more than 10. Thus, intrinsic variables are the best predictors: "Research activity is its own reward and is not engaged in for the sake of something else" (p. 28).

OTHER FACULTY ACTIVITIES

Although instruction and research represent the major missions of most institutions of higher education, data from a number of studies indicate that faculty members spend 15 percent to 30 percent of their time on a variety of activities other than teaching and research. Faculty attitudes toward those other activities vary greatly, and they are reflected in the time devoted to them.

Advisement and Interaction with Students

The amount of time devoted to counseling students varies widely—from an average of 1.8 percent of time (Ritchey 1959) to 12.4 percent (Bayer 1973). At three Florida institutions, the amount of time per week devoted to advisement ranged from 20 minutes to 17 hours (Raskin 1979). Some faculty members spend much time on campus, often with the office door open, willing to talk to anyone who drops in. Other faculty members are almost never available.

Some argue that faculty members do not devote enough time to advisement and that cost-effective procedures must be developed so that students will be given competent advice (Raskin 1979). It has occasionally been suggested that faculty members should be given released time for this activity (Bossenmaier 1978), but it is seldom done. Nor do most collective bargaining agreements specify advisement duties (Teague and Grites 1980), a further indication that many faculty members do not consider it important.

The amount of time devoted to advisement varies among both institutions and programs. Individualized degree programs require double the amount of counseling time needed by other programs (Hansen 1980). Only 15 percent of faculty members at four-year institutions devote no time to counseling, compared to 25 percent of those at community colleges, even though the presumably less academically sophisticated community college students need more counseling than those at four-year colleges (Stecklein, Willie, and Lorenz 1983).

Faculty members interact with students primarily as an instructor or academic advisor rather than as an equal discussing academic or intellectual matters or campus issues or engaging in informal socialization (Wilson, Wood, and Gaff 1974). The extent of instructor-student interaction is related to faculty members' belief that it is an important part of the educational process and to the extent to which faculty members keep their office hours. But the extent to which a faculty member interacts with students is not related to such factors as research productivity, research time, professional activities, or involvement in graduate teaching.

Faculty members spend less than 1 percent of their time working with student organizations; the percent is slightly higher at community colleges (Stecklein, Willie, and Lorenz 1983).

Some academics argue that advisement and counseling should be the responsibility of nonfaculty personnel, such as those in the office of the dean of students. Others suggest that nonfaculty cannot do the job as well as faculty. In either case, it is important to obtain data pertaining to the amount of time faculty members devote to interacting with students and the consequences of such interaction for both students and faculty members.

Consulting and Off-Campus Activities
Over the years, concern has been expressed that persons who engage in outside work may neglect their teaching duties, their students, or their institutional responsibilities. Faculty members have full-time jobs and, like executives, owe all of their time to the institution. Particular concern is apparent about persons who engage in private practice or paid consulting or who work for another organization (including another educational institution). Concern is less about unpaid consulting, which is assumed to benefit the institution or the community.

Ethical problems can arise when faculty members use institutional facilities while working on other than institutional business, particularly assignments for which they are paid. Off-campus faculty activities often involve the use of "materials" paid for by the institution: supplies and equipment, the telephone, the library, the computer center, for example. These costs are probably insignificant compared to the value of the faculty member's time lost to the institution. Faculty members who devote significant percentages of their time to noninstitutional business obtain a significant percent of their salary for work they are not doing.

Based on this reasoning, the University of Chicago for many years required faculty members to remit all of their consulting fees to the university, and some medical schools currently require faculty to remit at least a portion of their outside earnings. The seriousness of the problem is indicated by the fact that in 1976 the federal government asked Stanford University to reimburse it for all time that faculty members with federal contracts devoted to outside consulting (Patton and Marver 1979).

The problem is compounded by the normally vague definitions of faculty workload (Marsh and Dillon 1980). What is the normal work week of a faculty member? Most teachers in higher education say they work 50 to 60 hours per week. So do most nonacademic professionals, such as doctors, lawyers, and accountants (Dillon and Marsh 1979). How much professional time is paid for? Do faculty members, like college presidents, owe 168 hours per week to the institution? If a faculty member devotes an average of 55 hours per week to university work, can he or she devote additional hours to outside consulting? What about consulting during holidays and vacations? Is it reasonable for a faculty member to spend many hours per week on off-campus, paid activities?

In contrast to these concerns, consulting, whether paid or unpaid, helps institutions fulfill their public service responsibilities and enhance faculty members' competence (Allard 1982). Such activities are not excessive and do not take time away from other faculty activities (Marsh and Dillon 1980).

Many studies (for example, Bowen 1978; Ladd 1979; Marsh and Dillon 1980; Marver and Patton 1976) have reported that the percentage of faculty members who have outside income ranges from a low of 51 percent for faculty members on 11-month appointments (Bowen 1978) to a high of 85 percent for those on academic year appointments (Marsh and Dillon 1980). Marsh and Dillon believe that the figures reported in most studies are probably underestimated.

About 44 percent of faculty members earn additional income by teaching (Dunham, Wright, and Chandler 1966), with 12 percent of those teaching at institutions other than their own (Marsh and Dillon 1980). Between 10 percent (Marsh and Dillon 1980) and 17 percent (Dunham, Wright, and Chandler 1966) earn outside income from speeches and/or royalties, and 13 percent of faculty report income from consulting (Dunham, Wright, and Chandler 1966).

Consulting, whether paid or unpaid, help institutions fulfill their public service responsibilities.

Opportunities for consulting vary by discipline, rank, and institution. They are greatest in applied fields like engineering, business, medicine, and law. In one study, 21 percent of the Ph.D. faculty in the sciences and engineering engaged in consulting, compared to 12 percent in the humanities (Lewis and Boyer 1983). The percentage is greater at higher than at lower ranks (Bowen 1978; Lewis and Boyer 1983). Sixty percent of the paid consultants and one-third of the unpaid consultants are employed at universities, the rest by two- and four-year institutions (Patton and Marver 1979).

Faculty members who consult tend to have higher salaries and higher gross incomes than those who do not (Lewis and Boyer 1983). Faculty members who were paid consultants averaged 15 percent of their base in one study (Ladd 1979); those on academic-year appointments earned 19 percent over their base salary, and those on full-year appointments earned 11 percent (Bowen 1978). In another study, 93 percent of those with outside income said it was under 10 percent of their total income, compared to 2 percent who said it equaled at least 25 percent of their total income (Stecklein, Willie, and Lorenz 1983).

According to an article in the *New York Times* (12 September 1982), over 85 percent of the medical schools in the United States have regulations dealing with faculty income. The regulations are difficult to enforce, however, and the failure of the system and the large outside income of physicians who work at medical schools have been reported periodically. Of all academic physicians, 53 percent have private practices, double the percentage of full-time hospital staff physicians who have private practices (Goldberg 1969).

Similarly, the bylaws of the Association of American Law Schools (1982) are very explicit with respect to the duties of a faculty member: A "full-time teacher" in a law school is expected to devote "substantially" all of his time to being a teacher, scholar, and educator. Outside activities should not interfere with the person's regular presence and availability at the school; they should coincide with the major fields of interest to the person as a teacher and a scholar and when possible should provide enriching experiences that can be used in the person's capacity as a teacher and a scholar. Similar regulations in other disciplines might result in faculty members' spending more time on campus.

Institutional Service

"Institutional service" includes meetings, student services, other organized activities, and general administrative duties.

Meetings

All committee and group meetings—from a departmental subcommittee meeting to a universitywide faculty meeting—and the ancillary time devoted to preparing for meetings and writing minutes or reports for them belong in this category. Attendance at institutional functions—commencements, convocations, faculty teas, for example—could be included. The time spent in meetings of one kind or another can add up to a large number of hours per month (Yuker, Holmes, and Davidovicz 1972).

Student services

Definitions of "student service" vary. It includes "all services related to advising student programs and activities, directing student performances, and all other services for the student such as letters of recommendation" (Lorents 1971, p. 123), as well as the administrative and clerical time devoted to those functions, many of which belong to the category of interacting with students. Coaching an athletic team and directing the orchestra or a play can also be included (Manning and Romney 1973). It probably would be most useful if this category were restricted to specific *assigned* student service activities, including time spent working in the office of the dean of students, the counseling center, the placement center, the financial aid office, or the admissions office. Student-related activities that are not assigned should be placed in the category of interacting with students.

Other organized activities

"Other organized activities" refers to assigned duties outside the academic department not related to student services: assigned duties in the library, museum, research center, laboratory school, residence halls, bookstore, and so forth. Like student services, this category should be restricted to activities that are part of the faculty member's contractual assignment.

General administrative functions

"General administrative functions" includes institutional service activities that do not fit into the other categories: performing the duties of a department head, dean, vice president, or other administrative officer, recruiting faculty or students, keeping records, preparing budgets, allocating space, maintaining inventories, "pushing paper," and making nonpersonal telephone calls.

Some faculty members enjoy administrative duties; others detest and usually manage to avoid them. The average amount of time devoted to administrative duties ranges from a low of 8.2 percent (Bayer 1973) to a high of 21.2 percent (Orlans 1962).

The amount of time devoted to all categories of institutional service depends on the person, institution, discipline, and rank. At the University of Connecticut (1976), the range was from 3.8 to 13.7 hours per week. On the average, in one study, about 19 percent of faculty time was devoted to institutional service, approximately double the figure of 9 percent (about five hours per week) faculty members in the study perceived as ideal (Parsons and Platt 1969). Faculty in fine arts, education, and social work tend to devote relatively large amounts of time to institutional service, while those in the physical sciences, law, and engineering devote comparatively little time (University of Connecticut 1976). Full professors usually devote the most time to such activities, instructors the least (Hesseldenz 1976; University of Connecticut 1976). Rank has its drawbacks.

Fairchild (1981) reported that faculty spent 289 hours per year on institutional service—113 hours on correspondence and paperwork, 75 hours on travel to conferences, 40 hours on professional growth (usually listed as a separate category), 39 hours on meetings and committee work, and 22 hours on program development.

Public Service

Definitions of public service vary from one institution to another; they can include service to the community, to state and federal agencies, to foundations, and so forth

(Institute for Research 1978) but not activities unrelated to professional competence, such as membership in non-professional organizations, unless the institution requires them. Because faculty members sometimes are paid for those services, some institutions separate paid and unpaid public service.

Although the data indicate differences related to institutional type, discipline, and rank, these differences are minor, as faculty members devote only 2 to 3 percent of their time to public service. Faculty at four-year institutions devote about 4 percent of their time to public service, compared to about 1 percent at two-year institutions (Stecklein, Willie, and Lorenz 1983). Similarly, 58 percent of community college faculty report no time devoted to public service, compared to 36 percent of faculty at four-year institutions. Faculty at private institutions probably devote less time to public service than those at public institutions.

Differences among disciplines vary significantly. In one study, weekly hours ranged from an average of 6.0 in law to 0.3 in biology with (in descending order) social work, business, social science, education, humanities, physical science, fine arts, and engineering in between (University of Connecticut 1976). Using the Holland typology, Hesseldenz (1976) reported that faculty members in enterprising departments devoted 5 percent of their time to public service, those in social departments 4 percent, realistic 3 percent, investigative 2 percent, and arts 1 percent—results similar to those of the University of Connecticut.

Data pertaining to differences in rank are inconsistent. Hesseldenz (1976) reported no significant differences; each group averaged 3 percent. At the University of Connecticut, on the other hand, a positive relationship existed; full professors averaged 3.4 hours per week, associate professors 2.1, assistant professors 1.3, and instructors 0.3. These latter data appear more in accordance with theory and data on differences in rank in consulting and institutional service.

Professional Development

It is difficult to provide a precise, operational definition of the activities included in "professional development." Broadly defined, almost everything a college professor does could be considered to foster professional growth, which might account for the finding that most faculty members claim they work a 55-hour week. A narrow definition that distinguishes between activities directly related to professional growth and activities only peripherally related would seem more appropriate, however. Such a definition would include reading books and articles directly related to the profession, attending meetings devoted to one's profession, taking courses, and participating in faculty discussions on professional topics. It would exclude time spent reading newspapers and magazines, watching television, and engaging in general discussions.

Few estimates of professional development time are available, and most formulas do not include it as a factor (Miller 1968). Pessen (1962) claimed that it takes 14 hours per week to keep up with the literature, while Fairchild (1981) reported that professional development takes 2.2 percent of his yearly time. The average scholar in the humanities, sociology, and anthropology scans seven journals, regularly follows four or five journals, and reads three to five articles a week. Estimating 45 minutes each for four articles equals three hours per week. But, the same study reports, most scholars say they spend 10 to 12 hours per week reading books and journals, and 25 percent spend 16 hours or more. The data are contradictory.

With regard to meetings, 83 percent of the faculty in one study said they had attended professional meetings during the 1979–80 academic year, similar to the percentage for 1968 (Stecklein, Willie, and Lorenz 1983). Most faculty members had attended two meetings, and 27 percent attended three or more.

Differences undoubtedly result from individual inclinations as well as from differences among disciplines and possibly among ranks. Few data are available, however. Even though faculty members are expected to spend an appreciable (not defined) amount of time keeping up with the literature, no one appears to be interested in asking them how long it takes (Eagleton 1977).

Personal Activities
Personal activities include conversations, lunches, personal phone calls or errands, reading the newspaper, listening to the radio, taking a nap in the office, and so forth.

Activities can be classified in terms of whether they appear to be related to work or to personal interests, relaxation, or gossip (Ritchey 1959). Every faculty member in Ritchey's survey underestimated the time spent on personal activity.

This category is seldom included in studies of faculty workload, but the data presented in the two main studies in which it has been used (Lorents 1971; Ritchey 1959) should convince one that it should be included in all studies of faculty workload. Ritchey found that about eight hours (17.7 percent) of a 44-hour work week were devoted to personal activities, an indication of the surprisingly large percentage of time that faculty members devote to personal activities. It would be valuable if comparable time estimates could be obtained for other professions.

TOTAL WORKLOAD

This chapter addresses the heart of the issue. How hard do faculty members work? Does college teaching require more than 40 hours per week? Or does the typical faculty member have an easy life, teaching only six hours a week, about 35 weeks a year?

The data presented must be evaluated in the context of the earlier discussion. The reliability and validity of the data depend on the ways the data were collected. The length of the faculty work week depends on which workload categories were included and which excluded. The data indicate that differences among faculty members tend to be much greater than the similarities.

The Work Week

Many persons perceive the faculty work week as very short, because faculty members "teach" between three and 15 hours per week, with modal points around six and 12. To nonfaculty, this amount seems very little, particularly when one considers that the typical school year in higher education is about 35 weeks long. These perceptions probably account, at least in part, for the fact that many state legislatures have passed laws defining minimum workload standards for faculty teaching in public institutions (Bogue 1972). But thinking of a faculty member's workload as only teaching time is equivalent to defining a lawyer's workload in terms of only courtroom time or a legislator's time in terms of the hours spent on the floor of the legislature.*

Most faculty members say they work much more than 40 hours a week.

Most faculty members say they work much more than 40 hours a week. A review of over 100 studies concluded that faculty members typically work more than 50 hours per week (Interuniversity Council 1970), averaging 50 to 60 hours per week during the academic year. Similar data have also been reported at institutions in countries other than the United States (Onushkin 1972; Yuker 1977), which provides evidence of convergent validity. In view of all these data, faculty members say that on the average they spend about 55 hours per week during the academic year on academic and professional activities.

Despite the convergence, many persons at institutions of higher education—both administrators and faculty mem-

*J. E. Stecklein, personal communication.

bers—doubt that most faculty members work 55 hours per week, even when a broad definition of workload is used. Some react to the statement with disbelief, question the validity of the data, and state that most faculty members work a maximum of 35 to 40 hours per week, many fewer than 30 hours per week. Others believe that the data represent the true state of affairs and that most faculty members they know work more than 50 hours per week. Some people in this group complain that faculty members are overworked; others point out the extent of the professional commitment of most faculty members.

Critics state that even if faculty members do work over 50 hours per week, some of this work is not related to their professional position at a college or university, and time spent in activities, such as private consulting, should be excluded from faculty workload. They state that at least some of the convergence might be accounted for by the publicity given to statements about the 55-hour week of faculty members.

Data obtained by techniques other than faculty reports indicate that faculty work fewer than 55 hours per week, including 15 percent to 20 percent of the time that is spent on personal rather than academic activities (Lorents 1971; Ritchey 1959). But everyone spends some work time on personal activities.

Other data tend to confirm impressions that faculty work under 55 hours per week and that they work an average of 43 (median) to 44 (mean) hours per week, with the average ranging from 46 at research universities to about 36 at two-year colleges (Ladd 1979). Thirteen percent of all faculty say they work under 30 hours per week, 53 percent work 30 to 49 hours, 22 percent 50 to 59 hours, and 12 percent 60 hours or more.

The Work Year
The 55-hour week applies only to academic semesters. While faculty members may work during vacations and over the summer, they seldom claim that they put in the same number of hours that they do during the academic year. The total number of hours worked in 35 weeks spread over a more typical 48-week year would amount to approximately 40 hours per week, if faculty did no work over the summer. As many faculty members either do

research or teach during the summer, every 48 hours they work during the summer would add one hour to the 48-hour estimate.

Yearly data pertaining to faculty workload are scarce. Faculty members at the University of Queensland, for example, work an average of 2,119 hours per year, with averages ranging from 1,957 to 2,264 because of variations by rank and discipline (Fry 1981). Assuming a 55-hour week, that average turns into a 39-week year. Faculty members in nursing schools usually assume that they work eight or nine months, 34 to 39 weeks (Fawcett 1979). In academics, the nine-month year is as common as the 50-minute hour in psychotherapy.

The length of the work year is also affected by sabbaticals, which vary from institution to institution. Some institutions give faculty members a semester or a full year off every several (technically seven) years, providing them routinely to all faculty members who request them. Other colleges and universities make them available to only a portion of the faculty who meet specific criteria. On sabbatical, some faculty members work at least as hard as they normally do, while others engage in "intellectual renewal," better known as rest and relaxation. Not all faculty members who are eligible take sabbaticals. At the University of Minnesota, for example, only 38 percent of the faculty who could have taken sabbaticals had done so, although 6 percent of the faculty had taken three or more (Stecklein, Willie, and Lorenz 1983).

Faculty members differ in the time they spend on academic pursuits during periods when they are not teaching. A retrospective study at the University of California indicated that the average faculty member reported working a total of 55 hours during the 13 weeks of summer (Institute for Research 1978). Some faculty members, however, commented that they work very hard during the summer. Faculty in the sciences and engineering devote about 15 fewer hours per week to research in the summer, the same as during the regular school year (Lacy et al. 1981). Some put in additional time on research during the summer.

Perceptions of Faculty Workload
The claim that faculty members "spend about 55 hours per week in professional work . . . is probably an inflated fig-

ure, with 45 hours a more likely one'' (Mayhew 1979, p. 242). At the University of Connecticut, a sample of 31 students believed that faculty members work an average of 59 hours per week. Some graduate students estimated faculty work 50 to 70 hours per week, with advanced students giving higher estimates.

In the midtwenties, Kelly (1926) applied the standard 45-hour week common to union labor to faculty. Common use of this figure might help explain the prevalence of the 15-hour teaching load for many years and the concept that two hours of preparation are required for each hour in class. The drop to a 12-hour teaching load could then be seen as paralleling the decrease in the typical U.S. work week from 45 to 40 and currently 35 hours. A workload of 12 class hours corresponds to a work week of 36 hours if one assumes two hours of preparation for each hour spent in class. But with these ratios, it would be difficult to rationalize a workload of two graduate courses that meet for 1.5 hours per week each, unless one assumes many hours devoted to other duties.

A survey of 418 public junior and community colleges revealed that most expected faculty members to work a total of 30 hours per week (National Education Association 1972b). Only 27 percent of the institutions expected their faculty members to work 40 or more hours per week, and less than 3 percent expected 50 or more hours of work per week.

Few data indicate what faculty members consider as a full work week. In one survey, they considered about 42 hours to be a reasonable work week, and 20 percent said that faculty appointments should *not* be regarded as full-time responsibilities (McElhaney 1959). Perhaps many would agree with Simmons (1970), who assumed that a faculty member is paid to work only 40 hours per week.

Other Professions
In the comparison of professionals who are employed by institutions of higher education and professionals with similar training who work elsewhere, educators who work for the government average 1,680 hours per year (35 hours per week for 48 weeks), while those in higher education average between 1,584 and 1,782 (49.5 hours per week for 32 to 36 weeks) (Cornish 1972). Other data indicate that

academic persons employed in nonacademic settings work about five hours per week more than their colleagues in academic settings, but most faculty members, like executives, professionals, and others engaged in work that is relatively independent of time and place, "seldom put their work aside" (Thompson 1971, p. 4).

In academics, as opposed to other professions, no meaningful distinction can be made between work and leisure (although persons in other professions might disagree) (Blackburn 1974). Faculty members spend a lot of time with academic friends, talking shop, but other professionals do too.

Faculty are similar to persons in other occupations where individuals are independent workers without prescribed working hours (Institute for Research 1978). Such workers (for example, proprietors and physicians) tend to work about 15 hours a week more than regular employees because they tend to be more interested and more involved in what they are doing (Scitovsky 1976).

Even though faculty members report the same number of hours per week as other professionals, their salaries are lower. Faculty members on nine- or 10-month appointments earn 10 to 20 percent less than their counterparts who work for the federal government and 20 to 30 percent less than their counterparts in business, both of whom work 11 months (Bowen 1978). Part of the gap is closed by nonmonetary benefits, which are higher in education, and another part by outside earnings, which average 15 to 19 percent for faculty members on academic-year contracts and 11 percent for those with 11- or 12-month appointments. Faculty "may be better off than their counterparts in business or government" (Bowen 1978, p. 13).

Off-Campus Work
College teaching as a profession is characterized by the freedom it affords with respect to work time and work place. Except for scheduled class hours, a professor can work as many or as few hours as he wishes. Many activities (preparation for class, scholarly writing and reading, grading papers, for example) can be done on or off campus at any time of the day or night. As few faculty are on campus five days a week, and few are there more than eight hours a day, a substantial part of faculty work time must

be spent off campus. Off-campus time is spent at home, at other institutions, in research libraries and museums, and so on.

In one survey, faculty spent 10.8 hours (20 percent of total work time) on university business during other than business hours, defined as 8 a.m. to 12 noon and 1 p.m. to 5 p.m. Monday through Friday and 8 a.m. to 12 noon on Saturday (Ritchey 1959). Many college and university faculty members have classes only two or three days a week and do not appear on campus the other days. The fact that many faculty members do some of their work off campus may help to account for the skepticism with which some people view claims of a long work week, for a person who spends much time on campus is seldom chastised, even though the time may be wasted, but someone who spends little time on campus is often perceived as (and resented for) not being a hard worker or having well-paying consultantships.

Institutional Differences

The extent of institutional differences in workload is hard to assess because data reported by different institutions are seldom comparable as the result of differences in definitions, methodology, and procedures. Differences are found within various units of a state system (Lins 1971), and even larger differences can be expected in comparing unrelated institutions. Workloads in Ladd's study (1979) were inversely related to institutional quality; the lowest loads were at two-year schools, the highest at research universities. In another study, 70 percent of faculty at the highest category institutions spent under seven hours per week in class, compared to 37 percent in the middle category and 14 percent in the lowest category (Fulton and Trow 1974).

Differences among institutions in the amount of time faculty members devote to research has also been documented; one-third of the faculty in liberal arts colleges spend no time doing research, compared to 10 percent of the faculty in universities that receive large amounts of federal support (Orlans 1962). Thus, institutional differences are apparent in both the length and the components of the faculty work week.

Differences among Disciplines

The differences in workload among disciplines are probably relatively small compared to differences among individuals. For example, while English composition courses require more time than most courses (and some schools assign reduced teaching loads to persons teaching such courses) (Snepp 1968; Wilcox 1968), a 500-word essay can be graded in different ways. Some teachers do it in three minutes, while others take 30. The number and the length of assignments also vary. Thus, the average differences between disciplines are undoubtedly overshadowed by differences between individuals.

Rank

Although researchers do not completely agree on the relationship of rank to total hours worked, convergent data indicate a positive relationship. People who hold higher ranks work a few more hours per week than those at lower ranks. At the University of Connecticut (1976), professors averaged 57 hours per week with a decrease to 52 hours for instructors. Results were similar for faculty in Australia (Fry 1981) and Great Britain (Carter 1974). On the other hand, other data indicate no systematic differences between ranks (Bleything 1982; Hesseldenz 1976; Koos 1919). Still other data report a negative relationship; professors averaged only 56.6 hours per week, while instructors averaged 60.2 (Thompson 1971). While Thompson's data may coincide with prejudices, they contradict all of the other data. When differences are found, they are relatively slight—five hours per week, a 10 percent difference.

Gender

In 1974, Blackburn pointed out that even though gender had been compared with respect to specific aspects of workload, such as research activities, no studies of total workload had compared gender. A decade later, still only one or two studies have investigated the question. The University of Connecticut (1976) reported that male faculty members worked an average of 55.5 hours per week, females 52.0. At a large, private, midwestern university, women faculty members averaged 55 hours per week on professional work, exactly the convergent figure used to describe all faculty (Yogev 1982). (In addition, however, they spent an average of 35 hours per week on domestic work.) Comparable data for men are not available. More data on this topic are needed.

Individual Differences

The data indicating that faculty members work 55 hours per week reveal large individual differences. While few studies present frequency distributions or report measures of variability, those that do reveal a wide range in the number of hours worked (Koos 1919; Thompson 1971). These differences can be illustrated by assuming that during the academic year faculty members work an average of 55 hours per week with a standard deviation of 10 hours per week, which would indicate that two out of every three faculty members work between 40 and 60 hours per week and 95 percent of all faculty work 30 to 70 hours per week. This assumption seems reasonable, particularly if workload is defined as consisting of all of the components discussed in this monograph, including on-campus time devoted to personal activities.

Data indicate that individual workload data are skewed, with a small percent of faculty members devoting very much time to academic pursuits. These individuals produce a high percentage of the total academic output. Some "triple threat" faculty members work hard at and are very productive in teaching, research, and service (Fulton and Trow 1974), but such individuals are very rare and they are most likely to be found at the top-quality universities (Light 1974).

Professorial Prototypes

Differences among faculty members can be illustrated by a series of hypothetical descriptions—based on data presented in this monograph—of how faculty members at different institutions who differ in rank, discipline, gender, interests, and work habits might spend their working time. These descriptions represent statistical artifacts, and probably no real faculty members exactly fit the descriptions.

They can, however, provide some insight into faculty work habits.

Dr. G. Eliot is an associate professor of English at a well-known four-year liberal arts college. She teaches three courses a semester and has three hours released time to complete work on her second novel. Dr. Eliot devotes an average of 58 hours per week to academic work, with about 18 of those hours devoted to her courses and meetings with students. She devotes a few hours a week to correspondence and committee work in the department, but the bulk of her time is devoted to writing. She has published one novel and several book reviews. Her base salary is $31,000 per year.

Mr. J. Dewey is an instructor in the Educational Foundations Department of a large state university in the midwest. His teaching load is 12 semester hours. He works about 50 hours a week, with about 20 of those hours devoted to working on his dissertation. The other 30 hours are spent at the university, preparing for his classes, meeting with students, and participating in many committee meetings (which he believes will help when he comes up for tenure). He has not yet published anything, although his dissertation advisor predicts that he will be a prolific and important writer. His base salary is $21,000 per year.

Dr. C. Darwin is a distinguished professor of biology at a private university in the midwest. Although the normal teaching load is 12 hours, he has been successful in obtaining grants that pay for six hours of released time. He teaches only graduate courses and spends close to 40 hours per week in his laboratory and working with graduate students. He is well known in his field, having traveled widely and published many books and articles. His base salary is $55,000 per year.

Dr. S. Freud is an assistant professor of psychology at a community college. He usually teaches 15 hours a semester. He spends fewer than 25 hours a week on college work, devoting most of his time to his private practice in clinical psychology. But he also finds time to write articles. His current salary is $21,000.

Dr. M. Cassatt, professor of fine arts at a major university, teaches six or nine hours a semester and earns $47,000 per year. She spends about 20 hours a week at the university, some of which is devoted to her role as chairman of the university senate. Dr. Cassatt's paintings have been critically acclaimed and exhibited throughout the United States.

Mr. D. Jones is associate professor of finance at a medium-sized college. He has an M.B.A. and considers himself too busy to get a Ph.D. He is very much interested in his subject, is an excellent teacher, is advisor to the finance club, serves on the university budget committee, and is unofficial consultant to the finance committee of the board of trustees of the college. His salary of $32,000 is more than matched by his income from consulting. He has ideas for starting a financial news network.

IMPLICATIONS AND RECOMMENDATIONS

Many types of institutions continue to conduct studies of faculty workload for a variety of purposes. Some studies are carefully designed and carried out; others are not. Some achieve their purposes and yield useful results; others do not. The policy implications of some workload studies are not implemented because the results do not fit in with the prevalent myths of academia and the prejudices of faculty members and/or administrators. This situation is unfortunate because the data obtained in good studies are much more meaningful than myths and presumptions that are contradicted by data.

The following recommendations are based on the data presented in this monograph. They can help to increase the quality of the results obtained in workload studies, and they might even help in having the results taken seriously in making policy decisions.

1. A study that might be used to suggest or implement changes in workload should be conducted under the aegis of a joint faculty/administrative committee whose members agree on the purposes of the study and the methods to be used. This kind of sponsorship can help members of each group accept the validity of the results. Too often faculty and administrators perceive the purposes of workload studies differently; for example, faculty tend to want teaching loads reduced, while administrators want it maintained or increased. If representatives of both faculty and administration agree to the purposes and procedures, selective interpretation of the data is less likely.

2. The literature should be reviewed before any workload study, as with all scholarly research. The review might indicate that the study is unnecessary because the questions of interest have already been answered. Or it might indicate that the study's goals are unrealistic. The literature review can help ensure that no major methodological errors occur in the research.

3. In faculty surveys, the methodology should be developed and supervised by researchers who are familiar with survey research procedures in general and workload research in particular. The research should use measures whose reliability and validity have been demonstrated. The cover letter to the faculty should come from the committee and should urge the faculty's cooperation. Appropriate followup should be used to obtain the cooperation of the

Too often faculty and administrators perceive the purposes of workload studies differently.

greatest possible number of faculty members. Low rates of return can invalidate the study.

4. In recognition of differences among institutions, departments, and individuals, the presentation of the data should include measures of variability (for example, standard deviations) as well as averages (means or medians). Too often workload data are interpreted as representing "typical" faculty behavior without realizing that likely no faculty member actually behaves in the statistically typical fashion.

5. It should be recognized that institutions, departments, and individuals are frequently not comparable, except in general terms. Teaching loads that are appropriate at major research universities are not appropriate at liberal arts colleges, and they are definitely inappropriate at two-year schools. Workloads should be defined differently at different types of institutions; one should expect faculty at research universities to devote much of their time to scholarly productivity and expect community college faculty to devote most of their time to teaching and interacting with students rather than to research.

Differences between departments within an institution are often greater than differences between institutions. Professors of physics usually are expected to use their work time differently from professors of accounting or professors of fine arts. Research on workload must recognize these differences and attempt to measure them. A major problem arises when one attempts to equate the differences. Is one picture worth a thousand words in an article? Is a book the equivalent of a dozen articles? Such hypothetical questions and the attempt to develop workload formulas that specify equivalent work tend to be both arbitrary and meaningless. Is the work of Einstein equivalent to that of Beethoven, Freud, Jefferson, or Rodin? Rather than seeking equivalencies, we should define workloads in appropriate terms for each department. In view of these differences, attempts to develop standardized formulas with clearly defined workload equivalents are probably doomed to fail.

We should also recognize (and value) the existence of individual differences. Not all mathematicians, sociologists, or English professors are alike. Even though many more similarities usually exist among department members than between members of different departments, every large department has both workaholics and playaholics, teachers and researchers.

6. The data demonstrating the pervasiveness of individual differences in using time imply that basing faculty assignments on these differences could result in increases in work time and in productivity. The assignments could be based on a combination of effectiveness and interest. First, one could determine how effective a faculty member is in each of the assigned duties, such as teaching, research, working with students, administration, and so on. Then one could determine the extent of a faculty member's interest in each type of assignment, which could be done by workload studies, as data indicate that the relative amounts of time devoted to different activities tend to reflect the interests of the faculty member at least as much as they reflect specific assigned duties. Interest questionnaires could be used to validate the workload data. Tailoring faculty assignments to the individual's strengths and interests could lead to both increased productivity and increased faculty satisfaction. This approach is similar to management by objectives.

7. The complexity of the relationship between teaching load and scholarly productivity should be recognized. Although data indicate no overall relationship, the influence of other factors might be obscured. Thus, while an across-the-board reduction of teaching load will most probably not result in increased scholarship, increasing the load over 12 hours per semester probably will result in decreased scholarship. Similarly, decreasing the teaching loads of productive scholars might lead to increased scholarship, whereas decreasing the load of nonproductive faculty members seldom results in scholarly productivity. The data are quite clear about this point.

8. The relationship between teaching load and teaching effectiveness is probably similar to that between teaching load and scholarship. Previous research leads to the prediction that reducing the nonteaching assignments of faculty interested in teaching will probably result in their devoting more hours to teaching, while a reduction of nonteaching assignments for faculty who enjoy these assignments and do not enjoy teaching will probably not affect either the amount of time devoted to or the quality of

teaching. In other words, providing a faculty member with more time to engage in activities the person enjoys and is good at will result in increased productivity, while providing time for disliked or difficult activities probably will not result in greater productivity.

9. Additional studies that demonstrate how hard faculty members work are not needed. The data indicate faculty members' reports of their work time are similar to those of members of other professions. They say they work approximately the same number of hours per week. Some are dedicated, or workaholics, or both, and put in 70 or more hours per week. Some are more interested in other activities and devote minimum time to their work. Most seem to take their professional commitment seriously and spend their time appropriately.

10. Studies that demonstrate the validity of the data obtained in faculty workload surveys are needed, however. Such studies would ensure the quality of the data and help to convince skeptics that faculty members put in as many hours as they say they do.

REFERENCES

The ERIC Clearinghouse on Higher Education abstracts and indexes the current literature on higher education for the National Institute of Education's monthly bibliographic journal *Resources in Education*. Most of these publications are available through the ERIC Document Reproduction Service (EDRS). For publications cited in this bibliography that are available from EDRS, ordering number and price are included. Readers who wish to order a publication should write to the ERIC Document Reproduction Service, 3900 Wheeler Avenue, Alexandria, Virginia 22304. When ordering, please specify the document number. Documents are available as noted in microfiche (MF) and paper copy (PC). Because prices are subject to change, it is advisable to check the latest issue of *Resources in Education* for current cost based on the number of pages in the publication.

Adams, W. H. 1976. "Faculty Load." *Improving College and University Teaching* 24: 215–16 + .

Ahrens, Stephen W. 1978. "An Interinstitutional Analysis of Faculty Teaching Load." ED 180 324. 20 pp. MF–$1.19; PC–$3.89.

Allard, Sandra. 1982. *A Summary of Institutional Policies Affecting Outside and Offload Employment for Faculty at Maryland Public Higher Education Institutions*. Annapolis, Md.: Maryland State Board for Higher Education. ED 221 127. 24 pp. MF–$1.19; PC–$3.89.

Allison, P., and Stewart, J. A. 1974. "Productivity Differences among Scientists: Evidence for Accumulative Advantage." *American Sociological Review* 39: 596–606.

Anderson, C. H. 1968. "The Intellectual Subsociety Hypothesis: An Empirical Test." *Sociological Quarterly* 9: 210–27.

Anderson, Kenneth E. 1950. "The Relationship between Teacher Load and Student Achievement." *School Science and Mathematics* 20: 468–70.

Association of American Law Schools. 1982. *Association Information*. Washington, D.C.: Author.

Ayer, F. C. 1929. "Computing and Adjusting the University Teaching Load." *Nations Schools* 4: 26–30.

Ayre, D., et al., eds. 1981. *Resource Handbook on Manpower Flexibility Options in Ontario Universities*. Toronto: Ontario Institute for Studies in Education. ED 214 409. 427 pp. MF–$1.19; PC not available EDRS.

Bailey, D. 1968. "Faculty Teaching Loads: The State University." In *Faculty Teaching Loads in Colleges and Universities*. New York: Association of Departments of English. ED 017 528. 10 pp. MF–$1.19; PC–$3.89.

Baldridge, J. V.; Curtis, D. V.; Ecker, G.; and Riley, G. L. 1978.

Policy Making and Effective Leadership. San Francisco: Jossey-Bass.

Balfour, W. C. 1970. "The Academic Working Week." *Universities Quarterly* 24: 353–59.

Banks, J. 1963. "An Investigation of Methods for Determining Faculty Loads." Master's thesis, University of Alabama.

Bayer, A. E. 1973. "Teaching Faculty in Academe: 1972–1973." *ACE Research Reports* 8: 1–68. ED 080 517. 65 pp. MF–$1.19; PC–$7.39.

Behymer, C. E., and Blackburn, R. T. 1975. *Environmental and Personal Attributes Related to Faculty Productivity.* ED 104 317. 34 pp. MF–$1.19; PC–$5.64.

Biglan, A. 1973a. "The Characteristics of Subject Matter in Different Academic Areas." *Journal of Applied Psychology* 57: 195–203.

———. 1973b. "Relationships between Subject Matter Characteristics and the Structure and Output of University Departments." *Journal of Applied Psychology* 57: 204–13.

Billingsley, Andrew. 1982. "Building Strong Faculty in Black Colleges." *Journal of Negro Education* 51: 4–15.

Blackburn, R. T. 1974. "The Meaning of Work in Academia." In *Assessing Faculty Effort,* edited by J. I. Doi. New Directions for Institutional Research No. 2. San Francisco: Jossey-Bass.

Blackburn, R. T., and Trowbridge, K. W. 1973. "Faculty Accountability and Faculty Workload: A Preliminary Cost Analysis of Their Relationship as Revealed by Ph.D. Productivity." *Research in Higher Education* 1: 1–12.

Bleything, Willard B. 1982. "On the Workload of Faculty. Part I: Defining Faculty Workload. Part II. Elements of Faculty Workload and Their Relative Weightings. Part III. Faculty Load Formulas." *Journal of Optometric Education* 8: 6–22.

Bogue, E. G. 1972. "Method and Meaning in Faculty Activity Analysis." In *Reformation and Reallocation in Higher Education: 12th Annual Forum of the Association for Institutional Research,* edited by C. T. Stewart. Claremont, Calif.: Association for Institutional Research.

Bossenmaier, Monica M. 1978. "Faculty Perceptions of Academic Advising." *Nursing Outlook* 26: 191–94.

Bowen, Howard R. 1978. *Academic Compensation: Are Faculty and Staff in American Higher Education Adequately Paid?* New York: TIAA-CREF. ED 155 994. 139 pp. MF–$1.19; PC–$13.06.

———. 1980. *The Costs of Higher Education.* San Francisco: Jossey-Bass.

———. 1983. "The Art of Retrenchment." *Academe* 69: 21–24.

Bowles, Callie R. 1982. "The Teaching Practices of Two-Year College Science and Humanities Instructors." *Community and Junior College Quarterly of Research and Practice* 6: 129–44.

Brown, Stephanie L. 1979. "Approaching Faculty Productivity as a Mechanism for Retrenchment." In *Planning Rational Retrenchment.* New Directions for Institutional Research No. 24. San Francisco: Jossey-Bass.

Bunnell, K., ed. 1960. *Faculty Workload.* Washington, D.C.: American Council on Education.

Campbell, Colin. 1982. "An Empirical Model for Faculty Time Analysis." *Assessment and Evaluation in Higher Education* 7: 181–85.

Campbell, D. T., and Fiske, D. W. 1959. "Convergent and Discriminant Validation by the Multitrait-Multimethod Matrix." *Psychological Bulletin* 56: 81–105.

Caplow, T. 1960. "The Dynamics of Faculty Load Studies." In *Faculty Workload,* edited by K. Bunnell. Washington, D.C.: American Council on Education.

Carter, C. F. 1974. "Measuring Faculty Work in British Universities." In *Assessing Faculty Effort,* edited by J. I. Doi. New Directions for Institutional Research No. 2. San Francisco: Jossey-Bass.

Charters, W. W. 1942. "How Much Do Professors Work?" *Journal of Higher Education* 13: 298–301.

Cleghorn, M. P. 1930. "Report of Teaching Load Survey for the Engineering Division, Iowa State College." *Engineering Education* 20: 857–64.

Clemente, F. 1973. "Early Career Determinants of Research Productivity." *American Journal of Sociology* 79: 409–19.

Committee of Vice Chancellors and Principals of the Universities of the United Kingdom. 1972. *Report of an Enquiry into the Use of Academic Staff Time.* London: Author.

Conley, W. H. 1939. "The Junior College Instructor." *Junior College Journal* 9: 507–12.

Corcoran, Mary, and Clark, Shirley M. 1984. "Professional Socialization and Contemporary Career Attitudes of Three Faculty Generations." *Research in Higher Education* 20: 171–86.

Cornish, D. J. 1972. "Faculty Workloads—A Critical Examination." Edmonton: Alberta Colleges Commission. ED 607 065. 81 pp. MF–$1.19; PC–$9.56.

Creswell, John W. 1978. "Faculty Acceptance of a Workload Survey in One Major University." *Research in Higher Education* 8: 205–26.

Creswell, J. W., and Bean, J. P. 1981. "Research Output, Sociali-

zation, and the Biglan Model." *Research in Higher Education*
15: 69–91.

Creswell, J. W.; Kramer, G.; and Newton, T. A. 1978. *Faculty
Workload Provisions in Contract Agreements Negotiated at
Four-Year State Colleges*. Research Summary No. 6. Washington, D.C.: Academic Collective Bargaining Information Service.

Creswell, J. W., and Munsen, W. F. 1981. *Faculty Workload Pro-
visions in Negotiated Two-Year College Collective Bargaining
Contracts*. Washington, D.C.: Academic Collective Bargaining
Information Service.

Davis, C. O. 1924. "The Teaching Load in a University." *School
and Society* 19: 556–58.

Dillon, K. E. 1979. "Ethics in Consulting and Outside Professional Activities." Paper presented at the American Association for Higher Education annual conference, Washington,
D.C. ED 183 041. 7 pp. MF–$1.19; PC–$3.89.

Dillon, K. E., and Marsh, H. W. 1979. "A Comparison of Professional Earnings by Occupation: 1976." Paper presented at
the Fourth Annual Academic Planning Conference. Los An-
geles: University of Southern California, Office of Institutional
Studies.

Doi, J. 1961. "The Proper Use of Faculty Load Studies." In
Studies of College Faculty. Boulder, Colo.: Western Interstate
Commission for Higher Education.

———, ed. 1974. *Assessing Faculty Effort*. New Directions for
Institutional Research No. 2. San Francisco: Jossey-Bass.

Dorfman, L. T. 1980. "Emeritus Professors: Correlates of Professional Activity in Retirement." *Research in Higher Education*
12: 301–16.

Douglas, J. M.; Krause, L. A.; and Winogora, L. 1980. *Workload
and Productivity Bargaining in Higher Education*. Monograph
No. 3. New York: National Center for the Study of Collective
Bargaining in Higher Education and the Professions, CUNY,
Bernard Baruch College. ED 196 346. 38 pp. MF–$1.19; PC–
$5.64.

Dunham, R. E.; Wright, P. S.; and Chandler, M. O. 1966. *Teaching Faculty in Universities and Four-year Colleges: Spring
1963*. Washington, D.C.: U.S. Office of Education.

Durham, G. H. 1960. "The Uses and Abuses of Faculty Load
Data." In *Faculty Workload,* edited by K. Bunnell. Washington, D.C.: American Council on Education.

Dyer, Colin. 1978. "Study Leave and Other Research Time
Available to University Teachers in Australia, Great Britain,
France, and North America." *Vestes* 21: 18–25.

Eagleton, Lee C. 1977. "Faculty Workload Measurement at Penn State." *Chemical Engineering Education* 11: 130–33.

Eisen, C. L. 1976. "The Measurement of Job Satisfaction and Departmental Association at Western Kentucky University: Testing the Holland and Biglan Models." *Dissertation Abstracts International* 27: 655A.

Eurich, A. C., et al. 1981. *The City Colleges of Chicago Face the Eighties.* New York: Academy for Educational Development. ED 215 718. 226 pp. MF–$1.19; PC–$20.89.

Evenden, E. S.; Gamble, G. C.; and Blue, H. G. 1933. "Teacher Personnel in the United States." *National Survey of the Education of Teachers.* Bulletin No. 10. Washington, D.C.: Office of Education.

Fairchild, Thomas N. 1981. "Development and Utilization of a Faculty Time Analysis System: An Aid to Accountability in Higher Education." *Assessment and Evaluation in Higher Education* 6: 218–29.

Fawcett, Jacqueline. 1979. "Integrating Research into the Faculty Workload." *Nursing Outlook* 27: 259–62.

Feasley, C. E. 1978. "Faculty Workload Formulas in Competency-Based Programs." *Educational Technology* 18: 30–32.

Foley, A. L. 1929. "Report of Committee on Teaching Load in Colleges." *North Central Association Quarterly* 4: 250–57.

Fry, Neville H. 1981. "Academic Staff Work Loads in a University." *Journal of Educational Administration* 19: 93–105.

Fulton, O., and Trow, M. 1974. "Research Activity in American Higher Education." *Sociology of Education* 47: 29–73.

Gasson, I. S., and Otto, E. P. 1979. "Academic Staff Allocation Procedures in Institutions in Australia." *Vestes* 22: 52–54.

Geeter, Joan. 1981. "*The University of Connecticut* v. *the University of Connecticut Chapter of the AAUP:* Brief on Determining Faculty Workload in the Collective Bargaining Context." *Journal of College and University Law* 8: 254–67.

Goeres, E. R. 1978. "Faculty Productivity." *Collective Bargaining Perspectives* 3 (5). ED 167 020. 5 pp. MF–$1.19; PC–$3.89.

Goldberg, J. H. 1969. "How the Academic Physician Spends His Time." *Hospital Physician* 5: 61–65.

Goodwin, H. I., and Andes, J. O. 1974. *Collective Bargaining in Higher Education: Contract Content—1973.* Morgantown, W.V.: West Virginia University. ED 089 560. 121 pp. MF–$1.19; PC–$11.31.

Halsey, A. H., and Trow, M. 1971. *The British Academics.* London: Faber & Faber.

Hammons, J., and Schade, H. 1983. "A Museum Piece: Faculty Workload by Credit Hours." *Community and Junior College*

Journal 54: 37–39.

Hanesian, D. 1977. "Faculty Work Load Measurement at NJIT." *Chemical Engineering Education* 11: 134–38.

Hansen, E. U. 1978. "Advising Time Inventory." *The General College Studies* 15: 1–19. ED 172 839. 19 pp. MF–$1.19; PC–$3.89.

———. 1980. "The General College Individualized Baccalaureate Degree Programs: The First Decade of Experience." *Minnesota University General College Monographs* 1: 1–127. ED 197 691. 127 pp. MF–$1.19; PC–$13.06.

Harper, Ronald L. 1978. "Faculty Activity Analysis." In *Analyzing and Construction Cost*. New Directions for Institutional Research No. 5. San Francisco: Jossey-Bass.

Hauck, G. F. 1969. "Estimating Faculty Workload." *Engineering Education* 60: 117–19.

Henard, Ralph E. 1977. "An Examination of the Uses of Five Measures in Determining Faculty Workload." In *Research and Planning for Higher Education,* edited by R. Fenske. Claremont, Calif.: Association for Institutional Research.

———. 1979. *The Impacts of the Faculty Workload Emphasis on Postsecondary Education in the 1980s*. Paper presented at the annual forum of the Association for Institutional Research. ED 174 075. 21 pp. MF–$1.19; PC–$3.89.

Henle, R. J. 1967. *Systems for Measuring and Reporting the Resources and Activities of Colleges and Universities*. Washington, D.C.: National Science Foundation. ED 016 309. 454 pp. MF–$1.19; PC–$37.89.

Hesseldenz, J. S. 1976. "Personality-based Faculty Workload Analysis." *Research in Higher Education* 5: 321–34.

Hesseldenz, J. S., and Rodgers, S. A. 1976. "An Analysis of Predictors of Instruction Work Effort." *Research in Higher Education* 4: 219–34.

Hicks, J. W. 1960. "Faculty Workload—An Overview." In *Faculty Workload,* edited by K. Bunnell. Washington, D.C.: American Council on Education.

Hill, A. J. 1969. "Measuring Faculty Workload." *Journal of Engineering Education* 60: 92–96.

Hill, W. L. 1979. "A Comparative Analysis of Faculty Workload at II-A Universities." Report presented to the Teaching Load Ad Hoc Committee, Central Missouri State University. ED 176 687. 20 pp. MF–$1.19; PC not available EDRS.

Hilles, W. C. 1973. "Program Cost Allocation and the Validation of Faculty Activity Involvement." *Journal of Medical Education* 47: 805–13.

Hind, R. R. 1971. "Analysis of a Faculty: Professionalism, Evaluation, and the Authority Structure." In *Academic Governance,* edited by J. V. Baldridge. Berkeley, Calif.: McCutchan.

Hind, R. R.; Dornbusch, S. M.; and Scott, W. R. 1974. "A Theory of Evaluation Applied to a University Faculty." *Sociology of Education* 47: 114–28.

Hodgkinson, H. L. 1972. "Open Access—A Clue to Reformation and Reallocation." In *Reformation and Reallocation in Higher Education.* Claremont, Calif.: Association for Institutional Research. ED 089 557. 202 pp. MF–$1.19; PC–$18.72.

———. 21 May 1973. "A Truer Calculation of Faculty Workload." *Chronicle of Higher Education:* 7.

Holland, J. L. 1973. *Making Vocational Choices: A Theory of Careers.* Englewood Cliffs, N.J.: Prentice-Hall.

Holliman, Juanita M. 1977. "Analyzing Faculty Workload." *Nursing Outlook* 25: 721–23.

Hook, Colin M., and Rosenshine, Barak V. 1979. "Accuracy of Teacher Reports of Their Classroom Behavior." *Review of Educational Research* 49: 1–11.

Howell, C. E. 1962. "A Concept of the Measurement of Faculty Load." *Journal of Experimental Education* 31: 121–28.

Hoyt, D. P. 1974. "Interrelationships among Instructional Effectiveness, Publication Record, and Monetary Reward." *Research in Higher Education* 2: 81–88.

Huther, J. W. 1974. "Faculty Workloads in the State Capital." In *Assessing Faculty Effort,* edited by J. I. Doi. New Directions for Institutional Research No. 2. San Francisco: Jossey-Bass.

Institute for Research in Social Behavior. 1978. *University of California Faculty Time-Use Study: Report for the 1977–1978 Academic Year.* Berkeley: Author. ED 179 133. 98 pp. MF–$1.19; PC–$9.56.

Interuniversity Council of Ohio. 1970. *Faculty Load Study.* Columbus: Author.

Jedamus, P. 1974. "Teaching Loads over Time." In *Assessing Faculty Effort,* edited by J. I. Doi. New Directions for Institutional Research No. 2. San Francisco: Jossey-Bass.

Katz, D. A. 1973. "Faculty Salaries, Rates, Promotion, and Productivity at a Large University." *American Economic Review* 63: 469–77.

Katz, S. S., and Broker, L. 1974. "The Faculty Workload in Allied Health: Some Suggested Approaches." *Journal of Allied Health* 3: 104–8.

Keene, T. W. 1972. "Some Relationships between Class Contact Hours and Total Teaching Workload in Large U.S. Universities." Lakeland: University of Southern Florida.

Kelly, F. J. 1926. "Relative Amounts of Time Required for

Teaching Different College Courses." *Journal of Educational Research* 13: 273–83.

Knowles, A. G., and White, W. C. 1939. "Evaluation of Faculty Loads in Institutions of Higher Learning." *Journal of Engineering Education* 29: 798–810.

Koehler, J. E., and Slighton, R. L. 1973. "Activity Analysis and Cost Analysis in Medical Schools." *Journal of Medical Education* 48: 531–56.

Kojaku, L. K., and Zrebiec, L. 1983. "Equitability of Instructional Workload: Correlates of University Faculty Teaching Loads." Paper read at the convention of the American Educational Research Association, Montreal, Canada. ED 231 261. 12 pp. MF–$1.19; PC–$3.89.

Koos, L. V. 1919. *The Adjustment of the Teaching Load in a University*. Washington, D.C.: Bureau of Education.

Kuhn, T. S. 1962. *The Structure of Scientific Revolutions*. Chicago: University of Chicago Press.

Kutina, K. L. 1973. *Measurement of Faculty Effort: A Comparison of Data Collection via Percent Effort versus Activity Analysis*. Cleveland: Case Western Reserve University, School of Medicine, Operations and Analysis Office.

Lacy, L. E., et al. 1981. *Activities of Science and Engineering Faculty in Universities and 4-Year Colleges: 1978/79. Final Report*. Washington, D.C.: National Science Foundation. ED 221 129. 81 pp. MF–$1.19; PC–$9.56.

Ladd, E. C., Jr. 1979. "The Work Experience of American College Professors: Some Data and an Argument." *Current Issues in Higher Education*. Washington, D.C.: American Association for Higher Education. ED 193 998. 44 pp. MF–$1.19; PC not available EDRS.

Ladd, E. C., Jr., and Lipset, S. M. 1975. "How Professors Spend Their Time." *Chronicle of Higher Education* 11: 2.

———. 1977. *Survey of the American Professoriate*. Storrs, Conn.: University of Connecticut, Roper Center.

Laughlin, J. S. 1976. "A Sacred Cow: Class Size." *College and University* 51: 339–47.

Laughlin, J. S., and Lestrud, V. A. 1976. *Faculty Load and Faculty Activity Analysis: Who Considers the Individual Faculty Member?* Claremont, Calif.: Association for Institutional Research. ED 126 847. 15 pp. MF–$1.19; PC–$3.89.

Lee, E., and Kutina, K. 1974. "Sampling and Measurement Error in Faculty Activity and Effort Reporting." *Journal of Medical Education* 49: 989–91.

Leeper, P. 1984. "Universities Seek Ways to Soften Effort Reporting Requirement." *National Research Council News*

Report 34(8): 16–20.

Lewis, D. R., and Boyer, C. M. 1983. "Outside Professional Consulting and Faculty Vitality." Paper read at the meeting of the American Educational Research Association, Montreal, Canada.

Lienemann, W. H., and Bullis, B. 1980. "Collective Bargaining in Higher Education Systems: A Study of Four States." *AASCU Studies* No. 4. Washington, D.C.: American Association of State Colleges and Universities.

Light, D. W., Jr. 1974. "The Structure of the Academic Professions." *Sociology of Education* 47: 2–28.

Lindquist, Jack. 1978. "Social Learning and Problem Solving Strategies for Improving Academic Performance." In *Evaluating Faculty Performance and Vitality,* edited by W. R. Kirschling. New Directions for Institutional Research No. 20. San Francisco: Jossey-Bass.

Lins, L. J. 1971. *Characteristics and Utilization of Time of Teaching Faculty: University of Wisconsin and State University Systems.* Madison: Wisconsin Coordinating Council for Higher Education.

Lombardi, J. 1974. *Faculty Workload.* Washington, D.C.: ERIC Clearinghouse for Junior Colleges. ED 097 925. 25 pp. MF–$1.19; PC–$3.89.

Lorents, A. C. 1971. *Faculty Activity Analysis and Planning Models in Higher Education.* St. Paul, Minn.: Higher Education Coordinating Commission. ED 055 571. 350 pp. MF–$1.19; PC–$28.30.

McElhaney, J. H. 1959. "Attitudes of Selected Professors at Ohio State University Regarding Their Workloads." Ph.D. dissertation, Ohio State University.

McLaughlin, G. W.; Mahan, B. T.; and Montgomery, J. R. 1983. "Equity among Assistant Professors in Instructional Work Load." *Research in Higher Education* 18: 131–43.

McLaughlin, G. W.; Montgomery, J. R.; Gravely, A. R.; and Mahan, B. T. 1981. "Factors in Teacher Assignments: Measuring Workload by Effort." *Research in Higher Education* 14: 3–17. ED 189 961. 30 pp. MF–$1.19; PC–$5.64.

McMullen, L. B. 1927. *The Service Load in Teacher Training Institutions of the United States.* New York: Columbia University, Teachers College, Bureau of Publications.

Manning, C. W. 1974. *Faculty Activity Analysis: Interpretation and Uses of Data.* Boulder, Colo.: Western Interstate Commission for Higher Education. ED 100 232. 259 pp. MF–$1.19; PC–$22.64.

Manning, C. W., and Romney, L. C. 1973. *Faculty Activity Anal-*

ysis: Procedures Manual. Boulder, Colo.: Western Interstate Commission for Higher Education. ED 084 998. 146 pp. MF–$1.19; PC–$13.06.

Marsh, Herbert W., and Dillon, Kristine E. 1980. "Academic Productivity and Faculty Supplemental Income." *Journal of Higher Education* 51: 546–55.

Marver, James D., and Patton, Carl V. 1976. "The Correlates of Consultation: American Academics in 'The Real World,' " *Higher Education* 23: 319–35.

Maryland Council for Higher Education. 1975. *Faculty Activity Survey.* Annapolis: Author.

Matthews, D. 1964. "Family Recreation for University Faculty." *Journal of Health, Physical Education, and Recreation* 35: 33–35.

Mayhew, L. B. 1979. *Surviving the Eighties: Strategies and Procedures for Solving Fiscal and Enrollment Problems.* San Francisco: Jossey-Bass.

Meeth, R. L. 1974. "The Characteristics of Competency-Based Curricula." *Regional Spotlight* 9: 2–3.

Merton, R. K. 1968. "The Matthew Effect in Science." *Science* 159: 56–63.

Miller, K. C. 1968. "A Study of Faculty Workload in Higher Education." Ph.D. dissertation, University of Mississippi.

Mitchell, E. M. 1937. "Need for Time Analysis of Instruction." *Journal of Higher Education* 8: 311–14.

Mortimer, K. P., and Lozier, G. G. 1973. "Contracts of Four-Year Institutions." In *Faculty Unions and Collective Bargaining,* edited by E. D. Duryea, R. S. Fisk, and Associates. San Francisco: Jossey-Bass.

————. 1974. "Faculty Workload and Collective Bargaining." In *Assessing Faculty Effort,* edited by J. I. Doi. New Directions for Institutional Research No. 2. San Francisco: Jossey-Bass.

Morton, R. K. 1965. "Teacher's Job Load." *Improving College and University Teaching* 13: 155–56.

Muffo, J. A., and Langston, I. W. 1981. "Biglan's Dimensions: Are the Perceptions Empirically Based?" *Research in Higher Education* 15: 141–59.

Myers, Betty, and Mager, Gerald M. 1980. "The Emerging Professoriate: A Study of How New Professors Spend Their Time." ED 220 429. 22 pp. MF–$1.19; PC–$3.89.

Naples, C. J.; Caruthers, J. K.; and Naples, A. J. 1978. "Faculty Collective Bargaining: Implications for Academic Performance and Vitality." In *Evaluating Faculty Performance and Vitality,* edited by W. R. Kirschling. New Directions for Institutional Research No. 20. San Francisco: Jossey-Bass.

National Academy of Sciences, Institute of Medicine. 1974. *Report of a Study: Costs of Education in the Health Professions.* Washington, D.C.: Author.

National Council of Teachers of English, College Section. 1977. "Guidelines for the Workload of the College English Teacher." *College English* 38: 873–75.

National Education Association. 1972a. "Faculty Load Policies and Practices in Colleges and Universities." Washington, D.C.: Author. ED 068 029. 8 pp. MF–$1.19; PC–$3.89.

————. 1972b. "Faculty Load Policies and Practices in Public Junior and Community Colleges." Washington, D.C.: Author. ED 070 429. 5 pp. MF–$1.19; PC–$3.89.

National Science Foundation. 1967. *Systems for Measuring and Reporting the Resources and Activities of Colleges and Universities.* Washington, D.C.: Author.

————. 1981. *University Science and Engineering Faculty Spend One-Third of Professional Time in Research.* Washington, D.C.: Author. ED 207 830. 5 pp. MF–$1.19; PC not available EDRS.

Norman, C. 1981. "The Life and Times of an Academic Scientist." *Science* 214: 37.

Now, H. O. 1963. "The Effect of Various Factors on Faculty Workload at Findlay and Adrian College." Ph.D. dissertation, Ohio State University.

Onushkin, V. G. 1972. *Analysis of the Questionnaire of the Project "Planning the Development of Universities."* Paris: International Institute for Educational Planning.

Orlans, H. 1962. *The Effects of Federal Programs on Higher Education.* Washington, D.C.: Brookings Institution.

Over, R. 1982. "Research Productivity and Impact of Male and Female Psychologists." *American Psychologist* 37: 24–31.

Parsons, T., and Platt, G. M. 1969. "The American Academic Profession: A Research Proposal Submitted to the National Science Foundation." Cambridge: Harvard University.

Patton, C. V., and Marver, J. D. 1979. "Paid Consulting by American Academics." *Educational Record* 60: 175–84.

Pessen, I. 1962. "How Does the Professor Spend His Time?" *Junior College Journal* 32: 280–83.

Peters, Antoinette S., and Markello, Ross. 1982. "Job Satisfaction among Academic Physicians: Attitudes toward Job Components." *Journal of Medical Education* 57: 937–39.

Peters, D. S., and Mayfield, J. R. 1982. "Are There Any Rewards for Teaching?" *Improving College and University Teaching* 30: 105–10.

Raskin, M. 1979. "Critical Issue: Faculty Advising." *Peabody*

Journal of Education 56: 99–108.

Reeves, F. W., and Russell, J. D. 1929. *College Organization and Administration*. Indianapolis: Board of Education, Disciples of Christ.

Reeves, F. W., et al. 1933. *The University Faculty*. Chicago: University of Chicago.

Ritchey, J. A. 1959. "Utilization of Engineering Faculty Time." *Journal of Engineering Education* 50: 244–50.

Romney, L. C. 1971. "Faculty Activity Analysis: Overview and Major Issues." Boulder, Colo.: Western Interstate Commission for Higher Education. ED 062 947. 117 pp. MF–$1.19; PC–$11.31.

Ruml, B., and Morrison, D. H. 1959. *Memo to a College Trustee*. New York: McGraw-Hill.

Scitovsky, T. 1976. *The Joyless Economy: An Enquiry into Human Satisfaction and Consumer Dissatisfaction*. New York: Oxford University Press.

Sexson, J. E. 1967. "A Method for Computing Faculty Load." *Improving College and University Teaching* 15: 219–22.

Shay, J. E. 1974. "Coming to Grips with Faculty Workload." *Educational Record* 55: 52–58.

Shulman, C. H. 1980. "Do Faculty Really Work That Hard?" *AAHE-ERIC/Higher Education Research Currents*. ED 192 668. 5 pp. MF–$1.19; PC–$3.89.

———— . March/April 1981. "That Wonderful 12-Hour Work Week." *AGB Reports* 23: 15–19.

Siegfried, J. J., and White, K. J. 1973. "Teaching and Publishing as Determinants of Academic Salaries." *Journal of Economic Education* 5: 90–99.

Simmons, J. C. 1970. "What Is a Full-Time Equivalent Faculty Unit?" *College and University* 46: 33–36.

Smart, J. C., and Elton, C. F. 1982. "Validation of the Biglan Model." *Research in Higher Education* 82: 213–29.

Smart, J. C., and McLaughlin, G. W. 1978. "Reward Structures of Academic Disciplines." *Research in Higher Education* 8: 39–55.

Smith, Don N. 1979. "Survey of Workload and Compensation among English Department Heads at Category II-A Institutions." *ADE Bulletin* 61: 46–50.

Smith, Richard, and Fiedler, Fred E. 1971. "The Measurement of Scholarly Work: A Critical Review of the Literature." *Educational Record* 52: 225–32.

Snepp, D. 1968. "Teaching Conditions and Loads at San Francisco City College." ED 016 682. 7 pp. MF–$1.19; PC–$3.89.

Solliday, Michael A. 1982. "The University Supervisor: A Double Image." *Teacher Educator* 18: 11–15.

Starr, S. F. 1973. "A Fair Measure for Faculty Work Loads." *Educational Record* 54: 313–15.

Stecklein, J. E. 1960. "Methods of Analyzing, Expressing, and Reporting Faculty Load Data." In *Faculty Workload,* edited by K. Bunnell. Washington, D.C.: American Council on Education.

———. 1961. *How to Measure Faculty Workload.* Washington, D.C.: American Council on Education.

———. 1974. "Approaches to Measuring Workload over the Past Two Decades." In *Assessing Faculty Effort,* edited by J. I. Doi. New Directions for Institutional Research No. 2. San Francisco: Jossey-Bass.

Stecklein, J. E., and Willie, R. 1982. "Minnesota Community College Faculty Activities and Attitudes, 1956–1980." *Community and Junior College Quarterly of Research and Practice* 6: 12–19.

Stecklein, J. E.; Willie, R.; and Lorenz, G. E. 1983. *The Minnesota College Teacher Study.* Minneapolis: University of Minnesota Teacher Center.

Steinberg, Stephen. 1974. *The Academic Melting Pot: Catholics and Jews in American Higher Education.* New York: McGraw-Hill.

Stewart, L. O. 1934. "Teaching Loads: Their Measurement and Calculation." *Journal of Engineering Education* 25: 225–39.

Stickler, W. H. 1960. "Working Material and Bibliography on Faculty Load." In *Faculty Workload,* edited by K. Bunnell. Washington, D.C.: American Council on Education.

Stoddart, G. L. 1973. "Effort-Reporting and Cost Analysis of Medical Education." *Journal of Medical Education* 48: 814–23.

Sullivan, P. H. 1973. "Bias in Faculty Reports of Time and Effort Expenditure." In *Tomorrow's Imperatives Today,* edited by R. G. Cope. Claremont, Calif.: Association for Institutional Research. ED 089 559. 202 pp. MF–$1.19; PC–$18.72.

Swofford, R. 1978. "Faculty Accountability, Work Load, and Evaluation: A Synthesis." *Community College Frontiers* 6: 51–53.

Teague, G. V. 1981. "How Administrators Can Encourage Successful R&D." *Educational Record* 62: 36–39.

Teague, G. V., and Grites, T. J. 1980. "Faculty Contracts and Academic Advising." *Journal of College Student Personnel* 21: 40–44.

Thomas, A. L. 1982. "Reporting of Faculty Time: An Accounting Perspective." *Science* 215: 27–32.

Thomas, Wanda E., and Barker, Stephen C. 1983. "Developing a Workload Formula for High-Technology Faculty." Paper presented at the annual convention of the American Association of Community and Junior Colleges, New Orleans. ED 229 093. 36 pp. MF–$1.19; PC–$5.64.

Thompson, R. K. 1971. "How Does the Faculty Spend Its Time?" Mimeographed. Seattle, Washington: University of Washington.

Toombs, W. 1973. *Productivity: Burden of Success.* AAHE-ERIC Higher Education Research Report No. 2. Washington, D.C.: American Association for Higher Education. ED 076 174. 60 pp. MF–$1.19; PC–$7.39.

Tyndall, D. G., and Barnes, G. A. 1962. "Unit Costs of Instruction in Higher Education." *The Journal of Experimental Education* 31: 114–18.

University of Connecticut. 1976. *The Faculty Work Week at the University of Connecticut: Report by the Faculty Work Week Subcommittee.* Storrs, Conn.: Author.

University of Connecticut Board of Trustees. 1973. *Study of the Cost of Instruction and Faculty Performance and Accountability.* Storrs, Conn.: Author.

Walberg, H. J.; Strykowski, B. F.; Rovai, E.; and Hung, S. S. 1984. "Exceptional Performance." *Review of Educational Research* 54: 87–112.

Warden, S. A. 1974. "Socio-Political Issues of Faculty Activity Data." *Journal of Higher Education* 45: 458–71.

Wendel, F. C. 1973. "The Fifteen-Hour Work Week: Parkinson's Law at Its Best." *Educational Planning* 2: 22–27.

———. 1977. "The Faculty Member's Work Load." *Improving College and University Teaching* 25: 82–84.

Widom, C. S., and Burke, B. W. 1978. "Performance, Attitude, and Professional Socialization of Women in Academia." *Sex Roles* 4: 549–62.

Wilcox, T. 1968. "National Survey of Undergraduate Programs in English." In *Faculty Teaching Loads in Colleges and Universities.* New York: Association of Departments of English. ED 017 528. 10 pp. MF–$1.19; PC–$3.89.

Willie, R., and Stecklein, J. E. 1982. "A Three-Decade Comparison of College Faculty Characteristics, Satisfactions, Activities, and Attitudes." *Research in Higher Education* 16: 81–93.

Wilson, L. 1942. *Academic Man.* New York: Oxford University Press.

Wilson, R. C.; Wood, L.; and Gaff, J. G. 1974. "Social-Psychological Accessibility and Faculty-Student Interaction beyond the Classroom." *Sociology of Education* 47: 74–92.

Woodburne, L. S. 1958. *Principles of College and University Administration.* Stanford, Calif.: Stanford University Press.

Wyant, June F., and Morrison, Perry D. 1972. "A Faculty Workload Survey." *Journal of Education for Librarianship* 12: 155–61.

Yarborough, N. Patricia. 1982. "Taking a Look at Cost Effectiveness via Faculty Loads." *Community and Junior College Journal* 52: 21–24.

Yogev, Sara. 1982. "Are Professional Women Overworked?: Objective versus Subjective Perception of Role Loads." *Journal of Occupational Psychology* 55: 165–69.

Yuker, H. E. 1974. *Faculty Workload: Facts, Myths, and Commentary.* AAHE-ERIC Higher Education Research Report No. 6. Washington, D.C.: American Association for Higher Education. ED 095 756. 70 pp. MF–$1.19; PC–$7.39.

———. 1977. "Workloads of Academic Personnel." In *Encyclopedia of Higher Education,* edited by Asa S. Knowles. San Francisco: Jossey-Bass.

Yuker, H. E.; Holmes, J. A.; and Davidovicz, H. M. 1972. *Time Spent in Committee Meetings.* Hempstead, N.Y.: Hofstra University Center for the Study of Higher Education.

ASHE-ERIC HIGHER EDUCATION RESEARCH REPORTS

Starting in 1983, the Association for the Study of Higher Education assumed cosponsorship of the Higher Education Research
Reports with the ERIC Clearinghouse on Higher Education. For
the previous 11 years, ERIC and the American Association for
Higher Education prepared and published the reports.

Each report is the definitive analysis of a tough higher education problem, based on a thorough research of pertinent literature
and institutional experiences. Report topics, identified by a
national survey, are written by noted practitioners and scholars
with prepublication manuscript reviews by experts.

Ten monographs in the ASHE-ERIC Higher Education
Research Report series are published each year, available individ-
ually or by subscription. Subscription to 10 issues is $55 regular;
$40 for members of AERA, AAHE, and AIR; $35 for members of
ASHE. (Add $7.50 outside U.S.)

Prices for single copies, including 4th class postage and han-
dling, are $7.50 regular and $6.00 for members of AERA, AAHE,
AIR, and ASHE. If faster 1st class postage is desired for U.S.
and Canadian orders, for each publication ordered add $.75; for
overseas, add $4.50. For VISA and MasterCard payments, give
card number, expiration date, and signature. Orders under $25
must be prepaid. Bulk discounts are available on orders of 10 or
more of a single title. Order from the Publications Department,
Association for the Study of Higher Education, One Dupont Circle, Suite 630, Washington, D.C. 20036, (202) 296-2597. Write for
a complete list of Higher Education Research Reports and other
ASHE and ERIC publications.

1982 Higher Education Research Reports

1. Rating College Teaching: Criterion Studies of Student
   Evaluation-of-Instruction Instruments
   Sidney E. Benton

2. Faculty Evaluation: The Use of Explicit Criteria for Promotion, Retention, and Tenure
   Neal Whitman and Elaine Weiss

3. The Enrollment Crisis: Factors, Actors, and Impacts
   *J. Victor Baldridge, Frank R. Kemerer, and Kenneth C.
   Green*

4. Improving Instruction: Issues and Alternatives for Higher
   Education
   Charles C. Cole, Jr.

5. Planning for Program Discontinuance: From Default to
   Design
   Gerlinda S. Melchiori

6. State Planning, Budgeting, and Accountability: Approaches for Higher Education
   Carol E. Floyd

7. The Process of Change in Higher Education Institutions
   Robert C. Nordvall

8. Information Systems and Technological Decisions: A Guide for Non-Technical Administrators
   Robert L. Bailey

9. Government Support for Minority Participation in Higher Education
   Kenneth C. Green

10. The Department Chair: Professional Development and Role Conflict
    David B. Booth

1983 Higher Education Research Reports

1. The Path to Excellence: Quality Assurance in Higher Education
   Laurence R. Marcus, Anita O. Leone, and Edward D. Goldberg

2. Faculty Recruitment, Retention, and Fair Employment: Obligations and Opportunities
   John S. Waggaman

3. Meeting the Challenges: Developing Faculty Careers
   Michael C. T. Brookes and Katherine L. German

4. Raising Academic Standards: A Guide to Learning Improvement
   Ruth Talbott Keimig

5. Serving Learners at a Distance: A Guide to Program Practices
   Charles E. Feasley

6. Competence, Admissions, and Articulation: Returning to the Basics in Higher Education
   Jean L. Preer

7. Public Service in Higher Education: Practices and Priorities
   Patricia H. Crosson

8. Academic Employment and Retrenchment: Judicial Review and Administrative Action
   Robert M. Hendrickson and Barbara A. Lee

9. Burnout: The New Academic Disease
   Winifred Albizu Meléndez and Rafael M. de Guzmán

10. Academic Workplace: New Demands, Heightened Tensions
    Ann E. Austin and Zelda F. Gamson

1984 Higher Education Research Reports

1. Adult Learning: State Policies and Institutional Practices
   K. Patricia Cross and Anne-Marie McCartan

2. Student Stress: Effects and Solutions
   Neal A. Whitman, David C. Spendlove, and Claire H. Clark

3. Part-time Faculty: Higher Education at a Crossroads
   Judith M. Gappa

4. Sex Discrimination Law in Higher Education: The Lessons of the Past Decade
   J. Ralph Lindgren, Patti T. Ota, Perry A. Zirkel, and Nan Van Gieson

5. Faculty Freedoms and Institutional Accountability: Interactions and Conflicts
   Steven G. Olswang and Barbara A. Lee

6. The High-Technology Connection: Academic/Industrial Cooperation for Economic Growth
   Lynn G. Johnson

7. Employee Educational Programs: Implications for Industry and Higher Education
   Suzanne W. Morse

8. Academic Libraries: The Changing Knowledge Centers of Colleges and Universities
   Barbara B. Moran

9. Futures Research and the Strategic Planning Process: Implications for Higher Education
   James L. Morrison, William L. Renfro, and Wayne I. Boucher

10. Faculty Workload: Research, Theory, and Interpretation
    Harold E. Yuker

INDEX

1984
ASHE-ERIC
Higher Education
Research Report

This index provides access to the subject content of the 10 monographs in the 1984 ASHE-ERIC Higher Education Research
Report series. Entries are followed by a report number in bold
type and page numbers within a report. Entries with only a report
number indicate that the subject heading is the main focus of that
report.

model relationships, **6**:23–26
personnel exchange programs for, **6**:29–31
relationship to teaching, **10**:45–48
Research and development, cooperation between academe and
industry, **6**:15–37
Research centers, **6**:25–26, 33–36
Research enterprise of higher education, **6**:15–17, 20
Resource sharing, library collections, **8**:66–72
Retention, employee and sex discrimination, **4**:15–20
Retirement programs, **4**:26
Retraining of workers, **6**:72–73

S
Salaries
academic librarians, **8**:55–56
part-time faculty, **3**:70–72
sex discrimination, **4**:20–25
Scanning (see Environmental scanning)
Scholarship, relationship to research/teaching, **10**:45–48
Scientific misconduct, **5**:40–43
Sex discrimination law
admissions, **4**:40–45
affirmative action, **4**:31–35
athletics, **4**:51–55
benefits, **4**:25–28
employees, **4**:1–36
financial aid, **4**:45–47
hiring/retention/promotion/tenure, **4**:15–20
housing/parietal rules, **4**:50–51
indemnification, **4**:63
management control system, **4**:61–62
salary, **4**:20–25
sexual harassment, **4**:29–31, 47–48; **5**:38–40
student organizations/services, **4**:49–50
students, **4**:37–58
Title VII, **4**:11–15
tuition rates, **4**:45
working conditions, **4**:28–31
State coordination, adult learning, **1**:106–107
State law, sex discrimination, **4**:39
State planning, for technological development, **6**:11–13
State role
adult learning, **1**:119–127
economy, **1**:92–107

The numbers below refer to report number in the 1984 series.